DATE DUE

JAN. 8 1973		
June 20		

Bonsai for Pleasure

Bonsai for Pleasure

by Keiji Murata and
Takema Takeuchi

JAPAN PUBLICATIONS, INC.

Photographs by the authors, Ihei Misaki and Hideo Yukawa

Published by Japan Publications, Inc., Tokyo, Japan

Distributed by Japan Publications Trading Company
1255 Howard St., San Francisco, Calif. 94103 U.S.A.
175 Fifth Ave., New York, N.Y. 10010 U.S.A.
P.O. Box 5030 Tokyo International, Tokyo, Japan

Library of Congress Catalog Card No. 73–80051
First printing: December, 1969

Printed in Japan

Preface

No longer an exclusively Japanese craft, bonsai, known all over the world, enjoys the active participation of numerous groups and organizations including the Bonsai Association of Japan (former prime minister Nobusuke Kishi, honorary chairman) and other organizations in Europe and North and South America: there are fifty in the United States under the leadership of the New York Bonsai Association. Even specialists in the field are surprised at this amazing popularity, but there is a very good reason behind it.

Although mechanization has made our daily lives more comfortable, it has also produced environmental conditions in which humans tend to tire psychologically to the point of physical ill health. A return to the benefits of the sunlight and air of the natural world, however, can cure the ailment; and bonsai, by teaching the individual how to create from a natural plant gathered from mountains or hills, an ideal miniature tree of exquisite beauty, returns to human life some of the wonders of nature.

Since almost all lands, aside from regions of extreme cold, have the natural materials for bonsai cultivation, followers of the craft have definitely increased; and in this book we have attempted to explain actual bonsai techniques so that anyone anywhere can readily master them. I have treated theoretical matters, and my good friend Takema Takeuchi presents the technical aspects. Like me, active in contemporary Japanese bonsai affairs, Takeuchi, inheritor of the superlative technical skills of his late father Kiyomatsu Ueda, and well known for his work both at home and abroad, is possibly the best qualified man alive to teach the subject from a practical standpoint. Both he and I will be gladdened immeasurably if this book enables even one more person to acquire the skills requisite to an appreciation of the true joy of bonsai cultivation.

May, 1969

KEIJI MURATA

Contents

Gravure Illustrations

Color Photographs

I Categories

I. Characteristics

1. BONSAI AND TREES IN THE NATURAL STATE

Objects of appreciation produced by carefully training and modifying natural trees, bonsai, naturally impossible without borrowings from plants in the natural state, demand a sound understanding of the basic principles of growth and breeding. Because he is usually fond of bent and twisted trees, the bonsai specialists sometimes has to give considerable thought to the image of the shape he wants to produce. For this purpose, the trees growing in fields and mountains are a rich source of often enchantingly beautiful models. Furthermore, the very faults in natural trees frequently suggest ways to improve bonsai. In short, one of the most important points in bonsai cultivation is to select outstanding natural trees to emulate.

In their natural conditions trees must carry on life activities under a variety of environmental influences.

a. Climate—Light, Heat, Water, Wind

Because without it they would fail to assimilate carbon and produce organic life (photosynthesis), light is essential to all plants. For this reason, in contrast to the rich green foliage of trees in well lighted areas, the leaves of plants grown in dark places are pallid and sickly.

Most trees perish in environments that exceed their individual limits of heat and cold tolerance. For temperate zones, from 20 to 30 degrees Centigrade (68 to 86 degrees Fahrenheit) is the ideal range for optimum photosynthesis. The main component of the individual cell, water composes from 70 to 90 per cent of the entire bulk of most plants. The process of giving off through the surfaces of the leaves the water absorbed largely through the roots depends to a great extent on conditions of temperature and wind. For instance, much moisture is lost in hot windy areas, and moisture absorption is difficult in cold zones. Ideal conditions of temperature and wind produce optimum absorption and evaporation of moisture.

b. Soil—Topography and Soil Quality

The nature of the soil—the size of its particles and the amounts of water and nutrients it contains—influences the growth and development of plants.

c. Humans and Animals

Many animals assist in the distribution of the seeds of trees and other plants, but others, including man, often cause damage and mutilation.

Photosynthesis: Leaves and Branches

Generally, the growth of a tree is explained in terms of balance between production resulting from photosynthesis in the leaves and consumption resulting from respiration and falling leaves and branches. Under good lighting conditions a tree grows well because photosynthesis in the leaves far exceeds the amount of energy and matter consumed in respiration. On the other hand, trees in dark places fail to photosynthesize sufficiently and, consequently, wither and die.

Relationships between Maximum Wind and its Direction and the Trunks of Trees

To prevent excess loss of moisture and direct damage and injury, trees must assume a posture presenting minimal resistance to the winds that blow at nearly fixed seasons and velocities throughout the year in all parts of the world. This accounts for twists and slantings in pines by the seashores and in many other distinctive forms and markings in tree trunks in other regions.

Ideal Trees for Bonsai

No matter what their ages, trees assume individual shapes because of their natural environment. In addition, each species has its distinguishing characteristics, and good examples of all trees are usually available if the bonsai lover takes care to seek them out. To find the ideal tree for bonsai purposes, it is necessary to examine the finest examples of each type in nature and to make careful mental note of all its outstanding features. Later, the images thus created in the mind become guides in selecting and cultivating better bonsai.

2. BASICS OF BONSAI CULTIVATION

Ideally a bonsai is a dwarfed version of a tree whose main features—all but size—have already been determined in the natural state.

Selecting a Tree from Nature

The most important point is to seek a tree that is genetically capable of being dwarfed, even in the natural state. For instance, pines with short, profuse buds are traditionally held to be suitable.

Though it seems only common sense, it is always essential to stress the need for care in selecting a tree that lends itself to dwarfing: no matter how well you train and care for a plant, if it tends to grow fast and to develop wide, thick folliage, the bonsai will be a failure. It is, however, possible through crossbreeding to produce new, easily dwarfed strains.

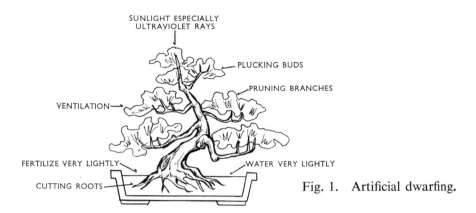

SUNLIGHT ESPECIALLY
ULTRAVIOLET RAYS

PLUCKING BUDS

PRUNING BRANCHES

VENTILATION

FERTILIZE VERY LIGHTLY

WATER VERY LIGHTLY

CUTTING ROOTS

Fig. 1. Artificial dwarfing.

Artificial Dwarfing

Though, since individual heredity and environment determine growth in nature, one might suppose a species that had apparently assumed a definite shape would remain unchanged, in fact, cultivation and care are of the utmost importance. Even a carefully chosen dwarfed specimen cannot manifest best form if neglected. The following points demand constant attention if a bonsai is to be always in peak condition.

    a. Sunlight

Generally speaking, strong sunlight effectively dwarfs plants because its ultraviolet rays impede growth: plants in high mountains exposed to the direct sunlight are small in stature. For this reason, it is good to keep bonsai out of doors on shelves where the sun reaches them all day.

    b. Ventilation

Good ventilation encourages evaporation from the leaves and thereby retards growth. Once again, the small mountain trees, as well as those in desert regions, bear witness to the validity of this rule.

    c. Soil

Naturally, the small amount of soil in the pot in which bonsai are grown restricts growth.

    d. Root Cutting

Cutting both the main root and the rootlets at transplanting time both stimulates the tree's metabolism and retards its growth.

Plant Physiology and Rules of Care

People who feel that dwarfing harms trees do not understand plant physiology. To stifle this mistaken preconception it is enough to say that instead of being malformations, bonsai represent some of the most beautiful, carefully tended, and hardiest specimens in the plant kingdom.

    a. Plucking Buds

The top bud of a plant is the strongest. In the natural state only this bud will grow vigorously, and those lower down will usually wither and die. In

Fig. 2.   Plucking the top bud. When the top bud is left in place, nutrients fail to reach the lower buds; when it is clipped, however, the lower buds become active.

bonsai, however, since the side branches are essential to balance, once the plant has taken firm root and is putting out new buds, carefully pinch off the top bud to stimulate growth in the others. In addition, should any bud, no matter what its location, seem to grow too fast, pinch it off to give the buds on other parts of the tree a chance to develop.

   b.   Cutting Roots

Because roots and the leaves and branches together effect a plant's growth, to dwarf the latter, begin by dwarfing the former. This means cutting the roots, particularly at transplanting time, not punishing them in some way to cause them to shrink. By absorbing large quantities of moisture the main root promotes the growth of vertical branches; consequently, to make the branches of a bonsai divide into smaller forms, cut the main root.

   By increasing the number of plant cells, cutting the roots causes division in the branches and leaves and a resulting denseness of foliage. At transplanting time, stimulate the further growth of side buds by cutting off the outer one-third of the smaller roots.

   Methods of bonsai care employ a plant's natural growth strength to achieve total balance in all parts.

Training Branches

In addition to trimming with scissors, pinching off buds, and cutting leaves, it is possible to improve bonsai shapes by wrapping branches with wire. Since the wire stops the nourishment intended for the branch at a point just above the wrapped area it contributes to retarding the plant's growth. If wrapped too tightly, however, the wire kills the branch: caution on this point is essential.

   The following methods employ the physiology of the plant to attain bonsai ends.

   a.   Strengthen the Plant to Achieve Balance among Parts

   Though, in the past, bonsai were created by punishing the tree and limiting its ability to grow, such an approach robbed the plant of its appeal. The modern method is to strengthen the plant as much as possible before attempting to achieve the necessary balance.

   b.   Accelerating Aging While Retarding Growth.

Because old tree shapes are bonsai ideals, to speed up the appearance of age, in many cases it is necessary to pinch off buds and prune leaves every six months and thus make—from the viewpoint of the tree's growing cycle—two years of one. Trained in this way, trees age more rapidly, but once they reach a certain age, excessive cutting and pruning are dangerous.

3. SOIL AND NOURISHMENT

Soil for Bonsai

Soil either promotes or impedes a plant's ability to grow. Particularly in the case of bonsai, where the amount of soil in the pot is strictly limited, it is a great mistake to assume with the uninformed that any soil will do.

a. Absorption Through the Roots and the Soil

Roots in the soil absorb water from which they take oxygen for photosynthesis and release carbon dioxide. If the roots become closely entwined in a confined area, absorption becomes difficult, and a harmful excess of carbon dioxide develops. To permit good ventilation a porous, granular soil is desirable.

b. Root Absorption Power and the Necessity for Porous Soil

Although roots absorb water and dissolved nutrients, not all water contained in soil is useful to plants. The only water supply available for effective absorption is capillary water, or that held by capillary action around the soil particles after the gravitational water—useless to the plant—has drained away. Consequently, no matter how much water it manages to retain, unless the soil is porous enough to permit capillary action, roots cannot absorb effectively. Coarse sand, however, allows water to flow away entirely, leaving the roots to desiccate.

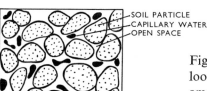

Fig. 3. Capillary water. Unless the soil is a loose conglomerate, openings will not form among the particles, and capillary absorption by the roots will be impossible.

c. Nutrients in the Soil

Together with water, the roots of plants absorb certain nutrient elements, present in slightly varying degrees in practically all soils: phosphorous, potassium, lime, etc. Since the amounts of these materials available in the limited soil in a bonsai pot is insufficient, fertilizers must sometimes be used. But they should never be agricultural chemicals, and they must always be applied in small quantities, because beauty, not size and productivity, is the aim in bonsai cultivation. Furthermore, too much fertilizer can injure the plant.

d. Summary

The following points are important in preparing soil for bonsai.

Good ventilation—tightly packed soil decreases the roots' absorption capability and reflects harmfully on the plant's physiology.

Good drainage—water standing in the bottom of the pot rots the roots. Both water and air must move freely through the soil.

Good water retention—bonsai are usually watered twice daily; for this reason a soil that has both good drainage and good water retention, like red clay, is preferable.

Moderate nutrition—fertilization only when needed.

Nourishment for Bonsai

Of the component elements in the vegetable body—water, carbon dioxide, hydrogen, oxygen, nitrogen, phosphorus, and potassium—all but the last three can be obtained from sunlight and the soil. Nitrogen, phosphorus, and potassium must be added to soils deficient in them: bonsai soil inevitably loses these important materials but fertilizers replenish the supply. Nitrogen is good for the leaves, and phosphorus and potassium help form blossoms and fruit.

The following three fertilizers are recommended:

(a) Oil cake

Made mostly from vegetable oils; providing nitrogen.

(b) Bone meal

Because of its high phosphorus content, good for plants that blossom or bear fruit; almost totally deficient in potassium.

(c) Vegetable ash

Used for its potassium content. One part ash from burned vegetable matter to nine parts soil provides a generous supply of lime and potassium.

II. Suitable Trees

Bonsai trees fall into two major classifications: conifers and a large group composed of miscellaneous trees bearing flowers or fruits, other shrubs, and sometimes even grasses.

1. CONIFERS

The pine, lovely to view all year round, long lived, and easy to train, has become so intimate a part of Japanese life as to be almost a symbol of the nation.

Always powerful, majestic, and weighty, the pine bonsai is especially impressive when old. Although most of the trees in this class are true evergreens, the larch is deciduous.

Evergreens commonly used in bonsai include the black pine (*Pinus thunbergii*), red pine (*Pinus densiflora*), *Nishiki* pine (a variety of black pine), five-needle pine (*Pinus pentaphylla*), silver spruce (*Picea jezoensis*), juniper

Trees Suitable for Bonsai

Evergreen Tree

Five-needle pine. The hardy short-needle pine lends itself to most bonsai shapes. In this instance, the slanted trunk and the outward thrusting lower right branch are good.

Deciduous Tree

Zelkova is one of the most popular deciduous bonsai trees because it is hardy and grows fast enough to produce satisfying results in a comparatively short time. This one is from seven to eight years old and has a four-inch trunk.

17

Flowering Tree

Azaleas make hardy, fast growing bonsai that please the eye with many flowers instead of ingeniously devised forms. This plant, a *Rhododendron lateritium*, in a slanted-trunk Kozan shape, may have either pale yellow or pink blossoms.

Fruit-bearing Tree

The Chinese quince is hardy, and its trunk thickens rapidly. Although it blooms with pale pink flowers, the tree is most highly prized for its light yellow fruit (slanted trunk style).

Grasses and Small Plants

Dwarfed *Ligularia* and small rushes from the fields and hills make pleasing bonsai.

Bonsai Shapes

Single Straight Trunk

1. Black Pine. Extremely masculine in mood, the shape of this tree is impressive because of the pleasing outward thrust of the lowest branch and because the trunk is visible for one third the height of the whole plant—an ideal proportion.

2. Zelkova. Many trees of this kind seem gentle because of their round, smooth trunks.

3.   Cryptomeria Cedar. This plant suggests a mighty,
old tree that, after battling with the natural elements,
has achieved grandeur.

4.   *Ficus retusa*. Never common, *Ficus retusa* bonsai
with clearly expressed forms, like this one, are extremely rare.

Single Straight Trunk

5. American Hemlock-spruce. Both the crypto-meria and the American hemlock-spruce must suggest age and strength against the forces of nature.

Slanting Trunk

6.   Silver Spruce. The lower right branch, thrusting backward to balance the left slant of the trunk, makes this an ideal shape.

7.   Hatchet-leaved arborvitae. The shape is natural, and the trunk leans only slightly.

8.   Black pine. The lower left branch reveals the distinctively roughened and peeling bark of this kind of pine.

Double Trunk

9. Silver Spruce. The thickness proportions of major and minor trunks and their pleasingly balanced lengths make this an outstanding tree.

10. Maple. The root spread is good, and the minor trunk harmonizes well with the powerful line of the main one.

11. Dwarf Wisteria. This is an excellent evocation of the shapes of natural trees in the fields.

Triple Trunk

12. Red Pine. Three trunks rising from the same root base: the major trunk is in the middle. The small trunk on the right is well formed.

Five Trunks

13. Five-needle Pine. Mountain forests frequently offer examples of groups of trees like this, which seem to have grown from seeds dropped by a single parent.

14. Five-needle Pine. This group suggests pines by the sea.

Bent Trunk

15. Black Pine. Trees like this, symbolic of the crushing weight of snows and the might of the winds, are more effective if areas of bark have been peeled away to expose the wood.

16. Japanese Cypress. The gentle mood of this cypress recalls the fields and plains.

25

Bent Trunk

17. Black Pine. The soft curve of the trunk contrasts with the rough texture of the bark.

18. Black Pine. The bend near the base is interesting, and the entire tree seems to be dancing elegantly.

Literati Form

19. Silver Spruce. Gently curving trunk, great height in proportion to spread, and few branches and leaves distinguish this refined and elegant bonsai form.

26

20. Silver Spruce. In groups of multiple trunks rising from the same root cluster, each member must contribute to the total balance. The trunk on the far right, however, by breaking away from the group, heightens the interest of the composition.

21. Five-needle Pine. This group is compact and pleasing; each minor trunk maintains a balanced relation with the main one.

Root-clump Groups

22. Maple. Group bonsai planted with stones subtly evoke a feeling of forest and grove.

23. *Euscaphis japonica.* In nature this tree frequently grows in groups from a single root.

Group Planting

24. Japanese Cypress. Many small trees, usually of the same kind, planted in a triangular arrangements suggest the depth and interest of groves and forests.

25. Silver Spruce. This composite of three grove compositions inspires an image of primeval forests.

26. Maple. An unusual grove composition with stones suggests a pond.

27. Beech. All of the trunks lean in the same direction, but the elaborate placement provides variety and depth.

Trees and Stones

28. Silver Spruce. Planting the spruce on a projection of a stone creates the feeling of a tree that has grown up fanned by sea breezes.

29. Silver Spruce. One of the many approaches to boulder-style bonsai, this composition suggests a deep mountain valley by means of several small silver spruces dotted over the surface of a rock.

30. Five-needle Pine. A rough stone with a skilfully placed pine represents a wind-blown island.

Connected Roots

31. Cryptomeria Cedar. These trees are carefully placed so that no two are the same distance apart whether viewed from the front or from the side.

Raft-style Connected Roots

32. Five-needle Pine. Similar in form to connected-roots style bonsai, these slanting and seemingly wind-bent trees, though artificially shaped after long years of cultivation, are equal in beauty to natural compositions.

OPPOSITE PAGE:

33. Five-needle Pine. Pines that bend down and then twist upward again and that show areas of stripped wood are rare.

34. Five-needle Pine. The lower right branch shifts the focus of the whole composition to a downward line; trees of this kind fall midway between the slanting-trunk and the full cascade styles.

Cascade

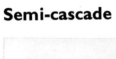

31

Twisted Trunk

35. Black Pine. Because they suggest that the winds and snows of ages have twisted them, the trunks of bonsai of this type must look rough and strong.

36. Black Pine. Though small, this tree has both strength and style.

(*Juniperus rigida*), Japanese cypress (*Chamaecyparis obtusa*), cryptomeria cedar (*Cryptomeria japonica*), Chinese juniper (*Juniperus chinensis*). Deciduous conifers used in bonsai are limited to the larch (*Larix leptolepis*).

2. MISCELLANEOUS TREES

The term "miscellaneous" describes all of the deciduous trees commonly put to bonsai use.

Fascinating because of their seasonal variety of spring buds, summer green, autumn red, yellow, and brown, and bare winter branches, the deciduous trees, possessed of more subtle trunks and branches than the evergreens, are also considerably more elegant in appearance. Some of the ones commonly used in bonsai are these.

Leafy Trees

Leafy trees prized largely for their colored autumn foliage and the loveliness of their forms after their leaves have fallen—maple (*Acer palmatum*), zelkova (*Zelkova serrata*), carpinus (*Carpinus laxiflora*), gingko (*Gingko biloba*), beech (*Fagus crenata*), ivy (*Parthenocissus tricuspidata*), wax tree (*Rhus succedanea*).

Other leafy trees prized largely for their greenery—willow (*Salix babylonica*), tamarisk (*Tamarix chinensis*).

Flowering Trees and Shrubs

plum (*Prunus Mume*), cherry (*Primula sinensis*), Japanese quince (*Pyrus Japonica*), aronia (*Malus halliana*), winter-flowering yellow jasmine (*Jasminum nudiflorum*), pomegranate (*Punica granatum*), wisteria (*Indogofera decora*), peach (*Prunus persica*), camellia (*Camellia japonica*), crepe myrtle (*Lagerstroemia indica*), sasanqua (*Camellia sasanqua*), rhododendron (*Rhododendron metternichii*), osmanthus (*Osmanthus asiaticus*), albizzia julibrissin), azalea (*Rhododendron lateritium*)

Fruit Bearing Plants

pomegranate (*Pumica granatum*), ilex (*Ilex serrata*), dwarfed apple (*Malus pumila*), akebia (*Akebia quinata*), persimmon (*Diospyros kaki*), apple, pear (*Pyrus serotina*), loquat (*Eriobotrya japonica*), silverberry (*Elaeagnus multiflora*), jujube (*Ziziphus jujuba*), Chinese quince (*Pseudocydonia sinensis*), bitter-sweet (*Celastrus orbiculatus*), rosewood (*Pterocarpus santalinus*), plum (*Prunus tomentosa*), gardenia (*Gardenia jasminoides*), nandina (*Nandina domestica*), mulberry (*Morus bombycus*), chestnut (*Castanea crenata*), horned orange (*Citrus medica*).

Grasses

Grasses are sometimes planted as bonsai arrangements to be appreciated for themselves or sometimes to highlight other bonsai.

adonis (*Adonis amurensis*), acorus (*Acorus calamus*), wild pinks (*Dianthus superbus*), *Hakonechloa macra*, rushes (*Phragmites communis*), ferns of many varieties, *Pecteilis radiata*, violets, Japanese pampas (*Miscanthus japonicus*), mealy primrose (*Hepatica triloba*), bamboo rushes, symphytum (*Omphalodes krameri*). The handsome *Rhodea japonica* and the many orchids, usually considered ornamental plants, are seldom used in bonsai.

III. Bonsai Forms

1. SINGLE STRAIGHT TRUNK

This form, consisting of a single main trunk rising vertically, roots spread in four directions, and front and back, right and left branches projecting harmoniously around the main trunk, must be balanced and stable.

The bottom or the second branch should project forward boldly, and the other branches and the trunk itself should decrease in projection toward the upper section of the plant. Two branches should never project right and left on the same level; neither should three or more be arranged radially on the same level. Ideally the finished plant should assume the form of an scalene triangle.

To achieve the dignity and masculinity of this form, often seen in pines and oaks growing in flat lands, it is important to let the branches begin at a point one third the height of the tree. The very simplicity of the style demands caution because a single ill shaped branch mars the beauty of the whole.

Trees suitable to this form include the following:
black pine, red pine, five-needle pine, silver spruce, juniper, cryptomeria cedar, Japanese cypress, Chinese juniper, zelkova, Chinese nettle (*Celtis sinensis*), azaleas, and maples.

2. SLANTING TRUNK

The main trunk rises on an angle to either right or left, the roots project most prominently in the same direction as the incline of the trunk, and the other branches shorten harmoniously toward the top of the tree. Bonsai in this form suggest high-rising seaside or mountain trees forced to lean because of the strong winds constantly buffeting them.

Not merely a tilted straight-trunk tree, the slanting-trunk style requires careful attention to branch proportions, balance among the supporting roots, and placement in the container to achieve the essential harmony. For instance, the roots must project most in the direction of the trunk slant, and the tree must be set in the pot so that the majority of open space is on that side too. Plants used in these arrangements include the black pine, red pine, silver spruce, five-needle pine, plum, and persimmon.

3. DOUBLE TRUNK

Two trunks rising from one root base, the major one tall and thick, the subordinate one shorter and more slender, suggest a well-matched, happily married couple. Ideally the subordinate trunk is one half the height of the major one, and both should rise close together at a sharp angle to each other. They must both stand boldly from a well spread root mass. In contrast to the magnificence of the straight-trunk bonsai, these trees generate a sense of warmth.

The following trees are commonly used in double-trunk arrangements: silver spruce, five-needle pine, cryptomeria cedar, plum, pomegranate, zelkova, and maple.

4. BENT TRUNK

Natural curves in both trunk and branches of a single-trunk bonsai create a mood of soft loveliness. The tree must rise well from a good spread of roots, and the branch projection must decrease toward the top of the plant. Trees with multi-dimensional curves are ideal, but fussiness in line is un-desirable. The first or second lowest branch should project boldly to one side. Curved forms occur often in nature in tall evergreens and deciduous trees.

A special variation of this form, the so-called literati style, makes full use of the natural characteristics of the plant and limits the number of branches and the amount of foliage to produce a bonsai extravagantly free yet elegant in tone. These trees make good bent-trunk bonsai: red pine, silver spruce, five-needle pine, plum, cherry, peach, maple, persimmon, dwarfed apple, ilex, willow, and tamarisk.

5. ROOT-CLUMP GROUPS

Though there is no limit to the number of trunks rising from a single root mass, they are generally in odd numbered quantities because anything in even numbers is difficult to balance. Assigning the role of major trunk to the largest and tallest and subordinating all the other to it produces the mood of a grove or forest. All the trunks grow from one root mass, but they should separate above ground level to give an impression of independence. Although all the trees must stand proudly and be clearly visible, the major one should be the most dignified, therefore, the most prominent. Using deciduous trees that take root well, it is possible to make cuttings from the root line and artificially produce multiple-trunk plants.

With the mellowing of age, these bonsai achieve fullness of form and the elegance of maturity. The following trees lend themselves readily to root-clump treatment; silver spruce, juniper, cryptomeria cedar, oriental arbor-vitae (*Biota orientalis*), Japanese cypress, beech, Japanese quince, azalea, maple, and rhododendron.

6. GROUP PLANTING

Once again, planted in odd numbers for ease of balance, any variety of trees or grasses, all of the same kind, or of different sorts, produce landscape symbolizations of mountains and deep valleys, forests, groves, tree-lined alleys, or mountain fields. The composite beauty of group planting gives fullest expression to the personality of the cultivator.

Although the problem does not arise in groups of homogeneous plants, when combining different varieties it is essential to select those that naturally require similar environments. For instance, a combination of trees that need abundant water and those that need little might well result in the dessication of one or the rotting of the other because watering to fulfill both demands is almost impossible.

As is true of the root-clump bonsai, in group planting the tallest, thickest plant must be the major point of interest, and all the others must be lower and more slender. Furthermore, too much foliage will spoil the effect; each plant must be clearly visible individually.

A wide shallow container is better than a deep one for group planting.

Use any of the following trees as well as many varieties of grasses, either together or separately: silver spruce, five-needle pine, juniper, cryptomeria cedar, zelkova, beech, or maple.

7. TREES AND STONES

These bonsai attempt to represent such natural scenes as the towering pine whose roots spread over the top of a boulder, red maples glimmering among the stones and mists of a waterfall, or the ancient evergreen growing among the rocks of an isolated island; in all these cases, without stones, the mood of the plants would suffer.

When bonsai are employed solely to emphasize the good points of the stones, the arrangement is set in a shallow flat basin containing water and sometimes sand. On the other hand, when the roots must embrace the stone, they are both planted in soil in a container of suitable depth.

Bonsai of this kind, traditionally divided into three components—container, stone, and plant—probably suit modern tastes better than any other and are the most interesting to learn. One must be cautious, however, to select trees whose roots take readily to being set on stone. The bonsai styles most often employed with stones are the bent trunk, slanted trunk, and semi-cascade. The stones themselves must be rough, irregularly shaped, and hard. Suitable trees include the silver spruce, five-needle pine, Chinese juniper, maple, azalea, cryptomeria cedar, and juniper.

8. CONNECTED ROOTS

Similar to root-clump bonsai in that many trunks rise from one root stock, the connected-roots style differs from the former in that the trunks, which suggest of rows of pines growing beside the sea, spring from a single root running more or less in a straight line. Either exposed or buried in the ground, this long root sprouts apparently individual trees along its length. The style derives from the shape of the unfortunate tree blown over by a wind storm and forced to alter the functions of its branches: those on the upper side of the fallen trunk become new trunks, and those on the underside develop into roots to supplement water intake. It is possible to artificially duplicate such running-root groves by covering the branches of of trees that tend to crawl along the ground in soil and stimulating them to put out new roots; The silver spruce and the five-needle pine are plants susceptible to this treatment.

Trees suitable to this style include the silver spruce, five-needle pine, juniper, cryptomeria cedar, Japanese quince, azalea, and maple.

9.   RAFT-STYLE CONNECTED ROOTS

In fact a sub-class of the preceding style, this is definitely an artificial arrangement in which the cultivator, by laying raft-like on their sides a number of trees whose branches and roots are unslightly or too regularly aligned to be interesting, forces them to develop new roots and trunks, in the connected-roots manner. Sometimes the results are surprisingly good, but arti ficiality is always apparent. With age, however, they mellow and improve.

Plants suitable to this treatment include the silver spruce, five-needle pine, cryptomeria cedar, Japanese quince, azalea, maple, and pomegranate.

10.   CASCADE

The main line of these trees, following the downward curve of the trunk and branches, cascades out of and below the side of the container; hence the name. Suggestive of natural trees growing on cliffs, by mountain streams or in deep valleys on large boulders, these bonsai project their trunks and main branches downward below the bottom level of the pot while maintaining balance with their upper sections. To achieve the proper mystic magnificence of cascade bonsai, select a deep container because shallow ones result in compositional instability. Plants suitable to this form include those, native to the mountains, which produce branches that crawl over the ground: black pine, five-needle pine, silver spruce, Chinese quince, pomegranate, ivy, wisteria, and such smaller plants as wild chrysanthemums.

11.   SEMI-CASCADE

Classifiable as midway between the slanting trunk and the true cascade, this form generally projects its trunk downward to about the level of the roots. In other words, it is as if a bent-trunk bonsai took a turn downward to extend its tip and branches half as far as those of a cascade.

Reminiscent of trees growing on inclines, the semi-cascade is both relatively easy to cultivate and pleasing to see; it escapes the heavy instability to which the true cascade is susceptible. Practically all of the usual bonsai plants can be treated this way: five-needle pine, silver spruce, maple, ivy, Chinese quince, pomegranate, persimmon, dwarfed apple, ilex, plum, peach, aronia, rose, hawthorn (*Crataegus cuneata*), wisteria, azalea, and rhododendron.

12. TWISTED TRUNK

Like old, gnarled trees forced by mountain snows or seaside winds to twist and turn their trunks into snaky shapes, these bonsai, even more elaborately curved than the bent-trunk style, usually have large exposed areas from which the bark has been worn away to show the naked wood beneath. Rich in variety and evocative of hoary age, twisted-trunk trees are popular.

Suitable plants include the black pine, red pine, five-needle pine, silver spruce, Japanese cypress, plum, wisteria, azalea and rhododendron.

2 Cultivation

I. Rules

Bonsai cultivation is not difficult, but there are a number of rules, formulated over many centuries of patient care and devotion, that facilitate breeding, cultivating, and raising ideally shaped trees without damaging the plants.

Most basic of all is the creation of environmental conditions harmonious with the needs of plants, which are, after all, living things with certain definite requirements. The following points, taken from old writings on the subject, are a basic approach to the development of a suitable plant environment.

1. Plants like the sun, but it must not be too hot.
2. They love the wind, but it must not be cold.
3. They love the rain but in moderation.
4. They love moisture but hate excess humidity.
5. They like dryness but cannot tolerate scorching.
6. They need soil but cannot be buried too deep.
7. They need fertilizing but not with unclean things.
8. They like warm air but cannot stand smoke.
9. They like people and hate insects.
10. They like being cultivated but want to be treated with respect.

Faithful adherence to these fine precepts will invariably bring good results.

II. Methods of Culturing

1. SEED

Of the many plants suitable to bonsai cultivation, several, whose seeds and fruits can be used directly, are often reproduced from seedlings, which transmit unaltered the characteristics of the parent stock. Seeding, because it produces many seedlings at one time, is an essential method in quantity production of high-quality trees. Although most trees have seeds large enough to be sown easily, it is always essential to provide three elements indispensable to their germination: water, oxygen, and, warmth—

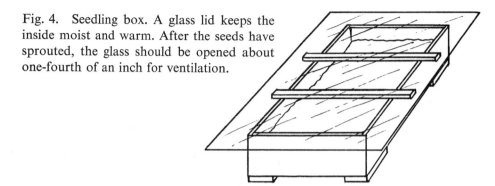

Fig. 4. Seedling box. A glass lid keeps the inside moist and warm. After the seeds have sprouted, the glass should be opened about one-fourth of an inch for ventilation.

generally higher than ten degrees Centigrade (fifty degrees Fahrenheit). For planting in the open ground, plow the soil well, breaking up all lumps, and, if it is the type that hardens easily, mix some river or mountain sand with it. After sowing the seeds, sprinkle a light layer of soil on them, and cover the ground with straw to prevent drying.

For a seed-germination container select a pot or other vessel with good drainage holes in the bottom. Use a mixture of fairly fine river sand and soil which has been sterilized by exposure to the sunlight.

Spread moderate gravel on the bottom of the container, and top it with a layer of the soil prepared as indicated above. Avoid excessively fine soils. When the container is seventy or eighty per cent filled with soil, sow the seeds; then cover them with a one-quarter- or one-half-inch layer of the same soil. Cover the bed with a plate of glass, about two or three inches above the surface of the soil, to keep the interior warm and moist. After the seeds have sprouted, raise or remove the glass for good ventilation.

In the case of very small seeds, spread sphagnum moss on top of the soil before sowing.

Sow seeds in the early spring. Grasses require about two weeks to germinate; conifers, such as the pine, about six weeks.

2. CUTTINGS

The cutting method, which also allows the propagation of many plants at one time, is superior to seeds in cases when seedlings do not transmit the best qualities of the parent stock. Although some trees, including the pines, do not usually make good cuttings, modern applications of plant hormones are increasing the rate of success even with difficult plants.

Cuttings, which should be put in the ground during a long period of warm, wet weather, such as the Japanese rainy period, may be new, or two-year-old branches cut to a suitable length, or pieces of root. In either case, however, if the cutting is excessively long, evaporation will be too great, and the cutting will not take root well. A good length for a cutting of azalea, for instance, is from three to four inches. In addition, clip away excess foliage from the scion. Cuttings should be kept at a temperature of from fifteen to twenty degrees Centigrade (fifty-nine to sixty-eight degrees Fahrenheit), in

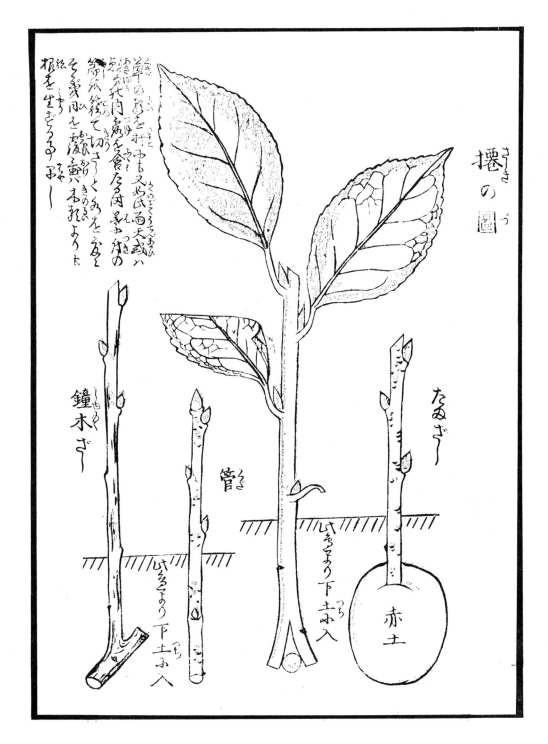

Fig. 5. Four methods of raising cuttings. The shaded horizontal line indicates the soil. This illustration is taken from *Sōmoku Sodategusa* (Plant-cultivation Manual), published in 1818.

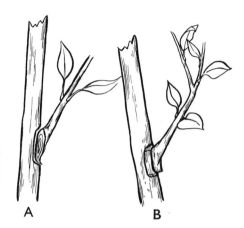

Fig. 6. Taking a cutting. (A) A thick section of the parent is cut off with the scion. (B) The scion is shaved closely from the parent.

A   B

a moist area in weak sunlight but good ventilation. They may be set out at any time from March till September, but until you are sure roots have emerged, do not expose them to dry, desiccating winds. Ideal scion lengths for easy care and good results are from two to four inches.

Shaving the scion close from the parent plant or leaving a little of the parent attached increases both the water intake of the cutting and its likelihood of survival.

Cuttings of bent branches produce twisted-trunk bonsai with strong roots.

Cut scions from the following plants in March: rose, crepe myrtle, nandina, forsythia (*Forsythia suspensa*), spindle tree (*Euonymus sieboldianus* Blume), willow, tamarisk, thunberg spirea (*Spiraea thunbergii*); from the following in April or May: cryptomeria cedar, Japanese cypress, and evergreen oak; from the following in June or July: azalea (both *Rhododendron indicum* and *Rhododendron lateritium*), sasanqua, camellia, maple; and from the following in September: Japanese quince.

To take cuttings from trees that do not root well—for instance pines— wrap wire tightly around the branch to cause an accumulation of nutrients just above the wrapping. After about three months of active growth for pines and three weeks for other trees, make a cut in the branch immediately

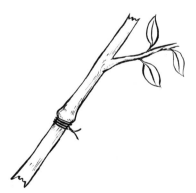

Fig. 7. Taking a cutting from a difficult plant. Wrapping wire around the branch so that in time a swelling develops at the top of the wrapped area makes taking a cutting easy.

above the wire; it will then put out roots from that area. If you have a greenhouse, this may be done at any time, but if you do not, work during rainy periods. (You will find that much of your bonsai activities take place then.) Roots should emerge from the cut in the branch in about three or four weeks; the cutting can be transplanted in about one year after this operation.

3. GRAFTING

Especially important when cuttings are impossible because the material is extremely weak, grafting often allows the propagation of outstanding trees that might otherwise be limited in number or lost.

Since botanically the graft will have the same characteristics as the stock, selection of the tree onto which to graft the scion is of the utmost importance. Always make the graft as close to the roots as possible because the connection between scion and stock is usually unsightly. Early spring, im-

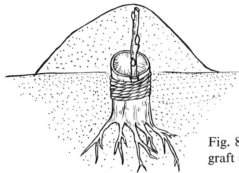

Fig. 8. Cover completely the scion of a top graft of deciduous tree for better growth.

Fig. 9. Side graft. The scion must be cut to fit into the slit in the parent. After being inserted, it is bound in place with twine.

(right)
Fig. 10. A pine tip graft. (from *Sōmoku Sodategusa*).

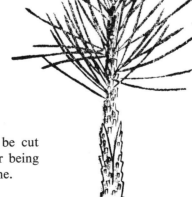

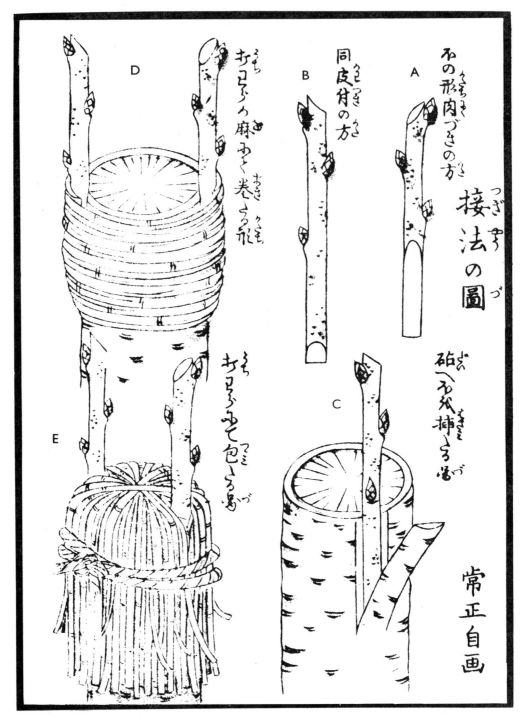

Fig. 11. Top grafting methods. *A* is a scion cut to join the parent on the inside, and *B* one to join on the outside. *C*, *D* and *E* show scions attached to parents, these drawings, too, are taken from *Sōmoku Sodategusa*.

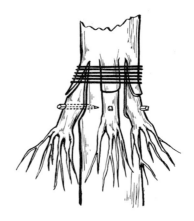

Fig. 12. Bud graft. This specialized grafting method requires that you make a cross-shaped cut in the bark of the parent, peel the bark back carefully, insert the bud, and fix it securely in place.

Fig. 13. Root graft. Wooden pegs and twine hold the scion root in place. When the two have grown together, cut off the lower section of the roots.

Fig. 14. The tree in the upper right has two top grafts enclosed in a frame of bamboo and rope filled with soil. The lower right plant shows a scion grafted to a root, and the one on the left a scion grafted to the trunk of a tree (from *Sōmoku Sodategusa*).

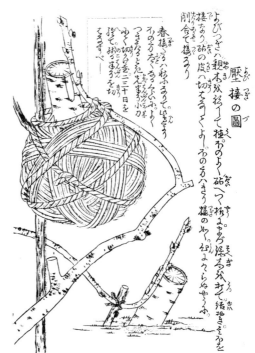

Fig. 15. Special grafting methods (from *Sōmoku Sodategusa*).

Fig. 16. Another special graft (from *Sōmoku Sodategusa*).

mediately before new buds become active, is the ideal time to graft whether the method is top grafting, used generally with deciduous trees, or side grafting, common with evergreens. Post-grafting care is similar to that given cuttings; that is, the plants should be kept in protective containers that shield from desiccating winds. But deciduous trees are best covered with soil until the scion has completely combined with the stock. Other grafting methods, such as the tip-grafting and the bud-grafting techniques, as well as a method for grafting roots instead of trunks or branches, require a high degree of technical skill. Root grafts permit quick multiplication of trees from which scions cannot be cut. Deciduous trees produce suitable scion material roughly four months after root grafting, but pines and other evergreens require longer: as much as two or three years in many cases. Grafted plants need constant watering; under no condition should they dry out.

4. LAYERING

Producing a dwarfed tree from seedlings takes a long time, but, of the means of asexually reproducing plants—layering, cuttings, grafting, and root division—the first is the only one that can develop a good bonsai fairly quickly. By layering and replanting a handsome branch from a garden tree, or unwanted branches from a bonsai whose shape requires correction, it is often possible to create surprisingly lovely plants.

To layer a branch from a deciduous tree, cut a ring of bark from the lowest part of the desired branch, make a serrate cut along the upper border of the exposed zone, wrap it in a packing of soil and moss, and water the wrapping frequently until roots appear—in from twenty to thirty days after the operation. For maples and cryptomeria cedars the branch may be cut off and replanted sixty days after the roots appear.

Though the evergreens take longer, wrapping a fine branch with wire, stripping a section of bark from it, packing it with soil and moss, watering

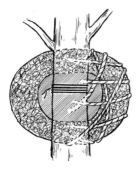

Fig. 17.   Layering pine or oak.
After wrapping the trunk or branch with wire to force the production of roots, continue as with other plants: pack soil around the wrapped section, cover this with dry moss, and secure the packing with rope.

(right)
Fig. 18.   Three methods of layering plants. The upper two drawings represent trees from which a section of bark has been removed to stimulate root growth. The one on the right is packed with clay wrapped in moss, and the one on the left with clay held in place with a section of bamboo and some twine. The written explanation says that wounding the bark of the tree causes roots to grow from the cut (from *Sōmoku Sodategusa*).

it often, and forcing an accumulation of carbohydrates in the wrapped zone will cause a generation of new rootlets from the exposed area. The roots should appear in two or three months after the stripping process, and the layer will be ready for severing and transplanting in one or two years after the appearance of the rootlets.

Though layering for most plants should be done in warm, moist seasons, when roots generate faster, some trees respond better to the treatment when it is carried out in early spring. For the time-demanding evergreens, make the layer whenever it occurs to you to do so except, of course, in winter.

The points on which to be especially careful in layering are these. Adequate water is essential at all times. Make the exposed area wide enough to prevent the two edges of bark from growing together and blocking the growth of roots, and expose the underlying wood in a complete ring around the branch to cause roots to generate evenly in all directions. Do not, however, wrap wire tightly around evergreens. Finally, avoid copper wire because it oxidizes and harms the tree.

5. ROOT DIVISION

Though sometimes employed, this method rarely produces good bonsai. It is customary to cut off small branches emerging from the bases of ordinary trees because they sap the strength of the parent: but for bonsai purposes, except in special cases, we seldom thin them and never divide the root mass.

In nature, trees often either divide their root masses to put out numerous separate trunks or, when afflicted with illness or insects, generate large numbers of branches near their bases. The bonsai cultivator, avoiding tools as much as possible, must separate the individual trunks one by one and tear the root mass with his hands for the following reasons. This method reduces the sizes of root wounds, and therefore minimizes wilting, lessens the amount of branch pruning necessary later, makes pleasing shapes easier to produce, and promotes rapid regrowth of bark. To facilitate this last process the wounds must be coated with pine rosin or some other waterproofing material free from chemical stimulants.

If tools are unavoidable, the roots will be easier to tear apart if you break them as nearly vertical as possible. The proper seasons for this operation are the ones in which transplanting is possible.

6. TREES FROM MOUNTAINS AND FIELDS

Grown under unfavorable natural conditions, many trees from the mountains are dwarfed enough to make good bonsai without further training. Although transplanting the deciduous trees, which root quickly and easily, requires no special technical skill, moving pines and other evergreens, which have deep main roots and a scarcity of rootlets near the ground surface, demands care and thorough preparation.

Working in the early spring, before buds appear on the trees, dig up as

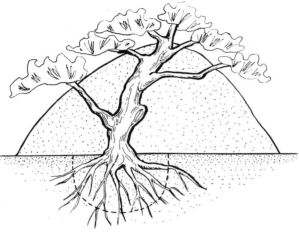

Fig. 19. Temporary planting of a tree taken from the mountains. Covering it with soil to the level of the small branches helps the tree take root fast.

Fig. 20. One year prior to the scheduled transplanting of a mountain tree, cut the peripheral roots. Leave the bottom roots untouched.

much of the main roots of the evergreen tree as possible. Plant it temporarily in a sunny part of a garden or field, and protect it by covering it with soil to the level of the small branches (Fig. 19). Water it often until it has taken root and is ready for proper planting. Deciduous trees will take firm root in about two months after being moved; evergreens require about six months. Though the problem is not serious in the mountains, lowland fields tend to be sunny, even in early spring, and it is, therefore, a good idea to cover the working area with an awning of some sort to prevent drying.

It is possible to remove trees from their natural settings in the autumn, but unless good facilities are available, the long winter and the necessary extra care reduce the chances of success.

For best results, when the tree to be moved is in a good environment, prepare a mass of rootlets (Fig. 20) the year before transplanting. In this case, too, frequent watering is important.

Remember to dig up as many rootlets as possible and to carry the plant so as to lose a minimum amount of root soil. Store natural trees in hothouses where the temperature can be kept at about eighteen degrees Centigrade (sixty-four degrees Fahrenheit) and the humidity at about eighty or ninety per cent.

A Collection of Famous Bonsai

1. YEW. Double trunk, rectangular container.

The good balance between the main and subordinate trunks creates the feeling of a single tree. The root spread is good, the bark is nicely roughened, and the total triangular shape preserves formal harmony.

2. BEECH. Straight trunk, rectangular container.

Beech is charming throughout the winter because it retains the yellow-brown foliage of late autumn. Blessed with an especially good root spread, this example is trained to suggest the trees true natural form.

49

3. ZELKOVA. Straight trunk, oval container.

The rhythmical placement of branches to right and left of the trunk in this balanced level form reveals how appealing deciduous trees can be even after their leaves have fallen.

(OPPOSITE PAGE, upper)

4. FIVE-NEEDLE PINE. Slanting trunk, rectangular container.

A truly mature tree of many years of age, this pine has achieved the ideal with its economical form, roughened trunk and branches, and curved tip, running in a direction opposite to the slant of the major section of the trunk.

50

5. CRYPTOMERIA CEDAR. Straight trunk, oval container.

Although the cryptomeria generally lends itself well to straight-trunk training, this tree varies from the standard by showing natural branch growth and patches of old foliage turned brown, as it does in the forest.

6. ARONIA. Slanting trunk, rectangular container.

This very old, downward blooming aronia has an interesting split in its trunk, which slants in a way perfectly suited to a condensed version of a natural tree.

7. CHINESE QUINCE. Triple trunk, rectangular container.
The pale yellow fruit of the Chinese quince is more highly regarded than its flowers. Though strong, fast growing, and relatively easy to cultivate, the quince rarely achieves the balance of form shown in this example.

8. JUNIPER. Coiled trunk, rectangular container.
Seemingly the veteran of hundreds of years of struggle with the elements, this juniper is especially appealing because of its bare trunk—almost half of the entire tree—and because of the graceful curve on the right.

52

9. FIVE-NEEDLE PINE. Curved trunk, rectangular container.

The short, dense foliage of this apparently old tree is extremely good. The moss at the base of the naturally shaped trunk is pleasing, and the lower branch successfully suggests depth.

10. ARONIA. Curved trunk, oval container.

A well-known version of the aronia, this old tree with a thick, well developed trunk has been trained to bloom with the flowers turned downward.

53

11. ILEX. Curved trunk, rectangular container.

A splendid burst of bright red, round berries, an economical curve in the trunk, and compact harmony in the branches make this an outstanding winter bonsai.

12. CHINESE JUNIPER. Coiled trunk, rectangular container.

This old and famous tree seems almost mystical because of the small area at the base which must absorb enough moisture to support the elaborately coiled upper section.

13. MAPLE (*Acer Palmatum*). Planted with
   stone, rectangular container.
More nearly planted on top of than with a
stone, the tree has a naturally formed triple
trunk composition, but its most outstanding
point is the root spread on the surface of the
rock.

14. ZELKOVA. Straight trunk, rectangular
   container.
The high-rising nature of the zelkova is extremely well expressed in this bonsai with its
excellent main branch division and dense
growth of smaller branches.

15. JUNIPER. Double trunk, round container.
Another famous old tree, this highly individual juniper has a white flame-like tip pointing skyward and providing the main point of emphasis.

16. BEECH. Group planting, oval container.
Beeches growing in the wild frequently occur in groves like this bonsai, in which technical display has been sacrificed to the creation of a realistic mood.

17. SILVER SPRUCE. Five trunks, rectangular container.
The foliage is dense and short, but the one trunk that breaks the continuity of the composition by leaning sharply from the others is the major source of interest.

18. JAPANESE CYPRESS. Group planting, oval container.
Skilful combining of open space and thirty-one trees and the placement of the center group to suggest perspective make this a new attempt in natural-grove-style group planting.

57

19. SILVER SPRUCE. Planted on a stone. Expressive of pines growing atop boulders in the mountains, this tree most powerfully reveals the upward striving of a plant constantly buffetted by wind and snow. The arrangement takes advantage of the peculiarities of an unusual piece of bonsai material.

20. FIVE-NEEDLE PINE. Connected-roots style, rectangular container.
Growing from a single connecting root, this bonsai evokes the mood of groves of pines by the sea. All of the subordinate trunks balance well with the major one, the fourth from the right.

21. SILVER SPRUCE. Planted with stone, rectangular container.

This apparently spontaneous growth of a seedling in a small amount of soil on a stone belongs to the bonsai category that prizes natural atmosphere.

22. DWARF APPLE. Slanting trunk, round container.

One of the best of all fruit-bearing bonsai, the dwarf apple is well represented by this old, thick-trunked tree, which has a fine crop of round crimson apples.

23. FIVE-NEEDLE PINE. So-called streamer form, stone used in place of a container.

The five-needle pine is easily trained to assume any form, even unusual ones like this, called a streamer because it seems to have been blown into the shape of a pennon by high winds.

Seedlings

(Below) Chinese quince: one year old (left), four years old (right).
(Right) Chinese quince grown from a seedling; eight years old.

Cuttings

Azalea (*Rhododendron indicum*) cuttings and a pot containing six-month old cuttings.

The cryptomeria cedar cuttings on the left side of the pot are four months old; those on the right are six months old.

GRAFT PREPARATION
1. A persimmon stock with trunk cut to allow the insertion of a graft scion.
2. Persimmon scion trimmed to match the stock plant exactly.
3. The scion tied securely to the stock with string.

Grafting

(Upper) A five-needle pine one year after grafting (right) and a black pine two years after a cut graft.
(Lower) A plum three years after a cut graft.

61

Layering

(From top to bottom)
1. Tree selected for bonsai use. A ring of bark has been removed from the trunk.
2. Red clay packed around the area from which the bark has been cut.
3. A layer of moss is added to the clay, tied with string, and watered.

A black pine, ten years after it was layered for bonsai use.

Wiring

A silver spruce before (above) and after (upper right) wire wrapping. The shape has been greatly improved by lowering the bottom branches. Paper-wrapped copper wire should be used. (Right) Beginning the wire-wrapping process.

(Below) Buttercup winterhazel (*Corylopsis spicata*, age five years) before wire wrapping. (Right below) After wrapping, balance with the branches on the left has been achieved by twisting the right branch in the opposite direction.

Bonsai Soils

(Upper row, left to right) pumice gravel, mountain gravel; (lower row, left to right) red loam, black loam, light, sandy clay.

Bonsai Pots and Trays

Glazed urn (Canton)

White glazed oval (*shirokōchi*).

Gray-black glazed oval (*namako*).

Reddish unglazed tray (*shudei*).

(Left) Light gray trough with inscription (*hakudei*); (right) purplish-gray trough (*shidei*).

Unglazed black trough (*udei*).

Purplish gray, deep trough (*arashidei*).

III. Shaping

1. NIPPING BUDS

Spring and summer, when plants grow most actively, are the seasons for correcting bonsai shapes by nipping excess buds. This is done by removing all buds except the reserve ones always found at the bases of leaves of both deciduous and evergreen trees. Constantly keeping the desired shape in mind, remove either two or three of the new buds from each branch, but if additional length is aesthetically pleasing, leave all buds in place, until the branch assumes the proper relationship to the mass of the tree.

After new pine buds have divided into five, three, or two needles, over a period of one or two weeks, remove all but five or six of the new needles. Do not nip new needles whose axial growth is poor. With red and black pines, instead of leaving five or six needles long, as is the case with most evergreens, it is best to cut all the needles short to force the development of new buds.

Nip the buds of cypress, cryptomeria cedar, juniper, silver fir, hemlock spruce (*Tsuga sieboldii*), white fir (*Abies firma*), and Chinese juniper from the ends of the branches; but as the trees grow large, it is important to keep reserve buds and reserve branches in mind while shaping and forming the plant.

Prompt and frequent bud nipping for vigorous maples and zelkova keeps the ends of the branches pliant and easy to train.

Unless the buds of fruit-bearing and flowering bonsai are either nipped short or left completely uncut and unpruned, the season for flower buds is absorbed in a redevelopment of leaf buds. Once buds are nipped, however, further trimming or pruning causes the loss of the flower buds.

A frequently employed technique for shortening black or red pine needles is to nip all of the buds in May or June and thereby to force the appearance of from two to five new buds on a single branch. This method should be applied only to strong trees that have been well fertilized.

Fig. 21. Bud nipping.

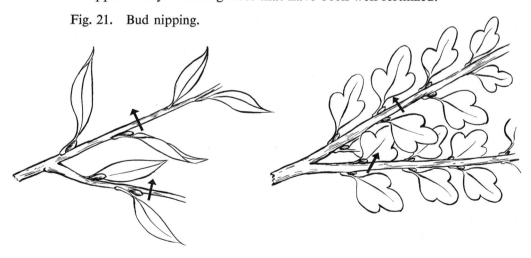

2. PRUNING

Bud nipping alone is insufficient to preserve the size and shape required of good bonsai. For this reason, in the early spring, before the new buds appear, pruning is essential both to balance the strength and weakness of the branches and to correct the shape of the plant. Once again, however, take care to preserve the vital reserve buds and branches. Furthermore, apparently severe cutting from the upper branches of a hardy, well developed tree actually prevents over-growth and the resulting destruction of the natural shape. It also helps create beautiful balance between the top and bottom sections of the tree. An old saying has it that good bonsai require pruning away of seven parts of the top to every three parts of the bottom. This, may overstate the case, but the upper branches demand more cutting than the lower ones.

The three basic methods of pruning, all of which should be used extensively, are these: shaping, while taking care to protect the reserve buds; removing all third branches from three-branch forks to produce only two-branch forks; and alternate cutting to shape the branches properly. The last method involves cutting so that no two branches oppose each other on the same level on different sides of trunk or main branch.

Azaleas, which grow fast and produce abundant foliage, must be pruned after each blooming. As is true of all similarly luxuriant plants it is easy to

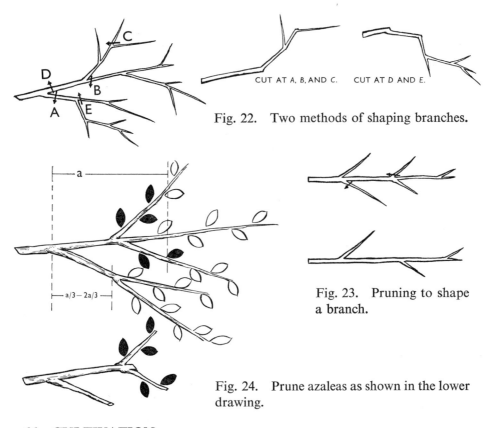

CUT AT A, B, AND C.   CUT AT D AND E.

Fig. 22.   Two methods of shaping branches.

Fig. 23.   Pruning to shape a branch.

Fig. 24.   Prune azaleas as shown in the lower drawing.

shape azaleas because in pruning one may cut away as much as one-third of the leaf bulk.

The thickness of foliage and branches in azaleas makes it impossible to pull them apart for selective trimming; consequently, random clipping is unavoidable. But in so cutting, arrange the lengths so that, after cutting, subordinate branches are one- or two-thirds the lengths of main branches.

In one or two weeks after trimming, two or three new buds will appear on the branches; these are very important to the plant's water intake. Unless pruning is accomplished by about the fifteenth of July, flowers will be inferior the following year.

Although each kind of tree makes slightly different demands, as a rule, unless one limits the amount of branch and foliage cut away to about one third the total, the balance between roots and leaves fails, and root rottage results. Furthermore, special care is needed on this point, because a plant that has been excessively pruned sometimes loses its recovery powers.

Removing all the new buds in August for black pines and in September for red pines inhibits the production of further buds that year but vastly increases the number developing the following year. This technique is widely used.

Prune and nip the buds from cryptomeria cedar and evergreen oaks in the late spring and again in the hot season, but never in cold weather.

Pruning is the operation that determines the future appearance of the tree: it is not merely cutting; it is a shaping process too.

3. TRIMMING LEAVES

When the new leaves of deciduous trees—maple, zelkova, etc.—have hardened, the plant has already made preparations for the succeeding crop of new buds. Consequently, at this time, it is possible to greatly increase the number of branches and buds, by cutting off all the leaves. Although, it is customary to carry out this procedure in rainy weather, any time when the

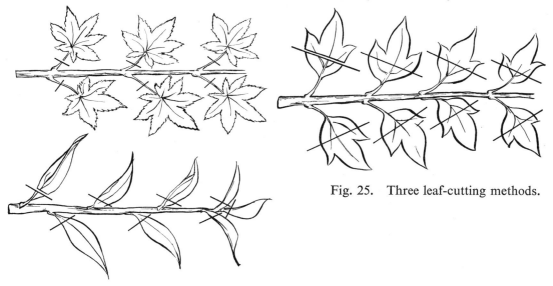

Fig. 25. Three leaf-cutting methods.

SHAPING 67

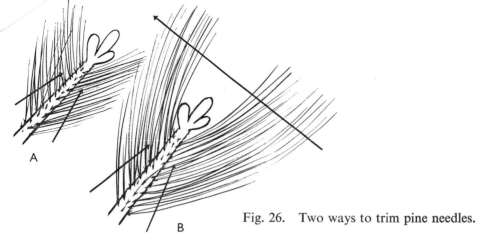

Fig. 26.   Two ways to trim pine needles.

plant is in a growth stage is suitable. Unless, however, the plant is fertilized before the leaves are cut, the new crop of buds will be inferior, and the tree may become diseased.

It is possible to improve the branches and shapes of old bonsai or of those with poor foliage without damaging the plant by thinning out one-half or two-thirds of the leaves. However even after application of fertilizer, if the plant seems in poor condition, leaf cutting may cause either few new buds or rotting of some of the branches: always govern the amount of pruning and cutting by the plant's condition. For example, though weak plants require caution, strong, young trees may be stripped of leaves as often as three times in a single summer.

Excess foliage in red and black pines interferes with ventilation and good lighting. To remedy the situation, either remove old leaves from the branch base (Fig. 26-A), or cut about one-third from the tips of the needles (Fig. 26-B). Five-needle pines, however, though permitting the removal of old needles from the branch base, will not tolerate cutting at the tips.

4. WIRING

If pruning and trimming are insufficient to produce the desired bonsai shape, it is possible to wire pliant, resilient seedlings and young trunks into pleasing shapes; but care should be taken to avoid curves that seem artificial. Wiring must employ the lines inherent in the plant; it must never be used to produce unnatural curves.

For pines and evergreens, which require their branches to be fixed in place for as long as two or three years to produce good shapes, the wiring must meet the following conditions. It must follow the lines of the trunk. It must be invisible from the front of the plant. It must be kept to a minimum. Wires, which must never cross, must be as fine as possible. To produce ideal plant shapes, keep all of these things in mind during the wiring process.

Wire for bonsai purposes, usually copper, comes in various thicknesses. To increase its flexibility to the required degree, it must be thoroughly heated before use.

Fixing the bottom end of the wire is the first and one of the most decisive

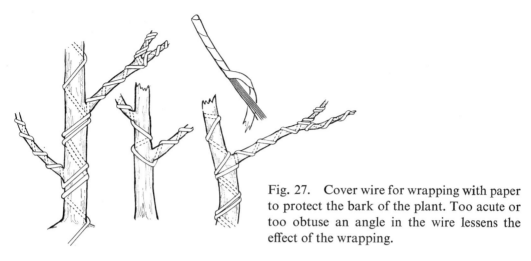

Fig. 27. Cover wire for wrapping with paper to protect the bark of the plant. Too acute or too obtuse an angle in the wire lessens the effect of the wrapping.

steps in the process. Instead of simply wrapping the wire around the tree, fix it so that it follows the line of the trunk or branch. For single trunks, bury the end of the wire in the soil and, working upward, wrap to the right for trunks that bend in that direction and to the left for those bending left. When branches are involved, add another wire at the fork of branch and trunk, and wrap each wire upward. Points at which the wire is fixed securely must be as few as possible. Wrap the wire lightly around branches and trunks to avoid injuring the bark. It is permissible to pass two strands of wire, but never three, over the same place.

Since shapes of the faster growing deciduous trees become permanent in about four or five weeks, wiring can be quickly removed. In these cases, paper-wrapped wire must be used to prevent damage to the delicate bark; the wiring should be loose and should follow the natural lines of the plant.

5. ESTABLISHING AN AXIS

Trees growing singly in the wild usually develop around the trunk line, which, extending from the roots to the tip of the plant, becomes the axis. Without such an axis the tree seems unstable and loses much of the strength of its appearance. The same thing is true of bonsai.

Although most plants develop axial lines quite naturally, in cases of bushy plants—the azaleas for instance—small branches sprouting from the root base often over-develop and thus obscure the true axis. In such cases, remedial trimming must be carried out at an early stage to prevent the destruction of the form.

Since the main trunk—the axis—and the tips of the branches are vigorous and grow rapidly it is best to prevent their over-development by leaving on them many buds and branches which, by dispersing the plant's energy among themselves, make concentration of strength and consequent excess growth impossible.

Should a plant lack an axial trunk, one can be made in a short time by selecting a branch in a suitable location, wiring it into a proper position, and stimulating it to grow strong and straight.

6. *JIN* AND *URO*

Jin is a word used to describe trees, the bark of the trunk or outsides of the branches of which has rotted exposing the wood beneath. *Uro* refers to an old tree that has been split by wind, snow, or lightning in such a way that the wood beneath the bark is not only exposed, but is also only half alive.

When it is necessary to remove top sections from plants that are too large, it is a good idea to make use of the resulting wound to produce the effect of a natural *jin*-style tree. A similar effect can be achieved with the hard trees—pines, etc.—without cutting, but since the deciduous trees, whose woods are softer, both rot and recover from injuries fast, it is necessary to apply some non-stimulant natural resin to the cut to prevent it from healing and thereby create the effect of natural decay. With the pines and evergreen oaks, whose hard woods recover from cuts slowly, make use of what would ordinarily be an unsightly, lingering blemish on the plant by shaping the wound to produce the effect of either a *jin* or an *uro*.

The *jin* appearance is produced by removing bark from the subordinate trunk near its tip. The wound must look as natural as possible. Furthermore, the subordinate trunk must be less than half the size of the main one. Specially thick trunks should narrow toward the top in three stages, branching improves the tree's appearance.

A similar method is used to take advantage of the wound left from cutting a large branch to create the loveliness of a naturally damaged and decayed tree of the *uro* kind.

7. CORRECTIONS

Today bonsai cultivators apply certain techniques and corrective measures during the process of assisting the tree to grow strong and healthy. Since bonsai raised from seedlings are common, in most instance, general corrective measures are part of the actual training of the plant. For the purposes of this book, however, I shall limit the meaning of "corrections" to those connected with major alterations in the plant shape.

Skillful use of steel rods for tying and bracing will enable the bonsai cultivator to freely correct the shape of almost any kind of trunk, but unless use

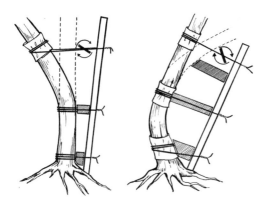

Fig. 28. Correcting the shape of a trunk.

Fig. 29. Two poles used to bend a trunk into an interesting shape.

is made of the natural curves of the plant, particularly in the cases of elaborately twisted bonsai, the results will be weak and unnatural.

Although, in the past, cuts, cross-shaped when viewed in section from above, were made in the trunks to facilitate bending into various shapes, this method is now little used.

Steel rods have long been employed in shape correction, and they are especially popular since seedlings lend themselves to this treatment.

IV. Training Bonsai

1. SINGLE STRAIGHT TRUNK

Bonsai of this type, patterned after the many beautiful straight trees in the wild, should be as natural in shape as possible, although, currently, some few cultivators are creating straight trunks of unnatural form.

Branches jutting from the straight trunk, for which it is important to select a plant well suited to this style, should never fork at the same level. A certain balance and order is essential in the placement of the branches from the bottom upward. Root spread should be in four, or preferably five, directions from the base of the plant. After you have chosen a tree that meets these conditions, do not become infatuated with the creative act. Instead, strive to produce the feeling of a natural tree.

This style is very easy to achieve with seedlings. Encourage the branches to grow and the trunk to thicken by repeated pruning until the tree is the desired shape.

Layering the top parts of garden plants or large bonsai will produce handsome single-trunk trees.

2. DOUBLE TRUNK

This style consists of two straight, bent, or twisted trunks, which must separate close to their bases and maintain an aesthetically pleasing size balance. The subordinate trunk must rise close to the main one, because too much space between their bases is ugly.

Although the scarcity of good material in the double trunk style means that most bonsai of this kind are the result of sectioning larger plants, with

Fig. 30. Double-trunk division: the two illustrations on the left are good; the one on the right poor.

a certain amount of time it is possible to produce lovely trees by grafting seedling branches or buds.

On the other hand, in layering a large plant, since it is possible to choose freely the spot where wire should be wrapped to force the development of roots, it is much easier to produce a number of forms, including those with three or five trunks.

Finally, the size difference between the two trunks should not be great; plants with small subordinate trunks fall into another category: the attached-offspring style.

3. BENT TRUNK

There are many outstanding examples of this style, the aim of which is to duplicate the majesty and beauty of old trees long subjected to winds and snows; in the mountains and other ill-favored environments much good material of this kind exists. Totally artificially produced twisted trunks, however, lack sharp curves and are, therefore, weaker in impact than natural ones. For this reason, it is imperative to take advantage of the knots and twists in plants to achieve the most successful effect.

Wiring is generally considered the most important corrective technique, but pruning can result in sharper, stronger curves. In fact, the lightning-bolt, continuous-curve bonsai cannot be produced in any other way. By repeated planned pruning from the seedling stage, forms very close to natural ones can be developed.

Long seedlings or cuttings can be trained to run around and through rods driven into the soil. In this way, elaborately curved bonsai can be produced. The rods will hold the plant in place as it grows into an interesting shape.

It is important to remark at this point, however, that application of only a single technique never produces a bonsai masterpiece. Even one curve in a trunk may require several different processes.

4. GROUP PLANTING

As most books on the subject relate, the greatest fault in this bonsai style is placing the trunks so that they fall in a straight line, overlap from certain vantage points, or produce branches that intersect with those of other trees. The plants should, instead, be placed to suggest that they all spring from one root mass. By using a fairly large number of plants and subordinating

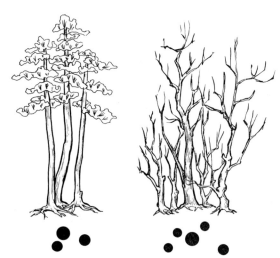

Fig. 31. No two trunks in group bonsai should be on a straight line when viewed from either front or side.

Fig. 32. Avoid the use of wire when connecting roots for a group bonsai.

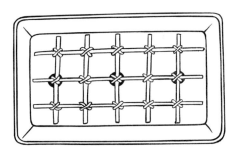

Fig. 33. This grid of slender sticks, used in connected-root bonsai, is fixed in place by means of twine run through the drainage holes in the bottom of the pot.

them all to one major trunk, it is possible to create a large bonsai arrangement in one vessel. Designed to make an attractive combination piece of plants unsuitable as individual bonsai, this style demands that all the trees be of the same type and approximately of the same age but as varying in size as possible. (Incidentally, there is a current trend to make group plantings of trees, each of which would be a handsome bonsai in its own rights.)

Tie the main root of the major plant to those of the subordinate and minor plants so that they form a pleasing ensemble, and plant them as you would any other bonsai. Since, depending on age and type, some plants have small main roots, tie the plants in position by making a lattice of slender sticks in the bottom of the pot and attaching the roots to it. These sticks can be held in place by means of cords run through the drainage holes in the pot bottom. The lattice increases the interest and freedom of plant placement. The planting itself is much like transplanting an ordinary bonsai, but because the process involves a great loss of root soil, it should be carried out only in the optimum season: sometime immediately before or after the vernal equinox. In the past, special mixed soils were used to hold the individual plants. This usage is no longer followed because the soil hinders the plants' growth and, when hardened, impedes water drainage.

Though they sometimes occur, group plantings of trees of different types are rarely successful, because plant strengths inevitably vary with the passage of time.

5. CONNECTED ROOTS

Group plantings of trees of the same kind, connected-roots bonsai are lovelier and easier to care for than the preceding group-planting style, but creating them requires more time and greater technical skill. Using a lattice of slender sticks in the bottom of the container and carefully selected seedlings or young plants with strong well developed lower branches, plant connected-roots bonsai just as group plantings. The roots and branches may be set in the desired positions and held in place by means of the lattice in the pot bottom. Prepare a pleasing group, developing around the central plant, and gradually each tree will generate new roots that grow together with those of neighboring trees.

Since the trunks and branches are tied in a horizontal position, the trees will emerge at an angle. Insert small stones to correct this.

At present, instead of the old-fashioned method of using fallen trees, from which roots have gradually developed along the side of a trunk lying in contact with the ground, it is customary to section a horizontal branch and force it to generate roots along its length. Another interesting connected-roots bonsai can be produced by forcing the subordinate trunk of a double-trunk plant to lie on the ground and thereby generate roots along its length. The resulting tree is both powerful and beautiful.

Thorough attention to the stick lattice in the bottom of the container is the most important aspect of preparations. Furthermore, use only stones to direct the developing trunks because copper or steel wires can injure the young bark. If tying is essential, use hemp rope or plastic cords instead of wire.

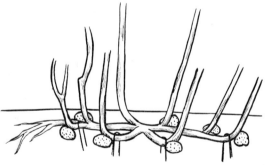

Fig. 34.   Use small stones as fulcrums against which to bend the trunks of connected-root bonsai. These roots are tied with twine to the stick frame shown in Fig. 33.

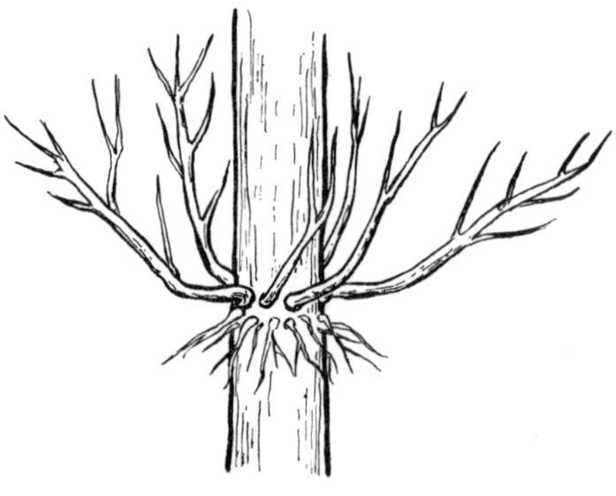

Fig. 35.   Taking a section from a trunk with two or three branches emerging at roughly the same level enables you to develop a well shaped bonsai.

6. RAFT-STYLE CONNECTED ROOTS

This style so closely resembles the preceding that in some instances distinguishing between them is difficult. In general, however, the raft style results when a lower branch of a tree grows into the ground near the root base of the parent. Since this downward growth curves and twists the trunk of the main plant, the raft style often adds appeal to an uninteresting, straight-trunk bonsai. The method of planting is identical with those for the group and connected-roots style. Once again, avoid the use of wire and of ordinary string, which rots too quickly. Hemp ropes are best because they last well and hold the trunks and branches in the desired positions.

Since the plant must be forced downward, at the beginning set the largest roots in a corner of the pot so that the new trunks will be in the center.

7. CASCADE

Evocative representations of trees hanging over mountain cliffs and leaning into valleys, this style may be used for pines, evergreen oaks, or any of the deciduous trees. In the last case, the seasonal variety of foliage intensifies the beauty of the plant. For best results, select trees with a preponderance of branches on one side, with roots spreading largely in one direction, with large curves at the bases, or with curved trunks.

The cascade style may be subdivided into two categories: the pure cascade, in which the lowest tip of the cascading branch is lower than the level of the bottom of the container; the semi-cascade, in which the tip of the lowest branch is approximately on a level with the bottom of the pot.

Since the roots play only a small role in the beauty of cascade bonsai, deep containers are used for them, but semi-cascades are more interesting when planted in standard, flat, tray-like containers. Careful selection of the container for semi-cascades is of the greatest importance.

Although it is not a true cascade style, the literati hanging bonsai deserves attention for its striking loveliness.

8. TREES AND STONES

Life force is so strong in plants that beauty is often found thriving under the most adverse conditions. Each bonsai type has its own charm, but those with rocks combine the best of both the plant and the stone to recreate a special feeling of trees in deep mountain ravines or on high, sheer cliffs.

The three general types of bonsai with rocks are as follows:
(1) Those in which the roots of the plant run along grooves in the rock surface and then into the soil in the pot.
(2) Plants whose roots are fixed to the irregularities of rough-surfaced stones set in shallow trays of water.
(3) Plants attached to flat stones because they are visually unsuited to potting.

Firmly fixing these plants in place on the stone is unavoidable because the soil available for roots to grip is extremely limited in amount. This is accomplished by attaching fine hemp cords to the small grooves in the stones by means of lead wedges. The cords are then used to tie the roots of the plant in position.

After temporarily setting the plant, apply a coating of the following soil preparation: four parts sphagnum moss, three parts river sand, and three parts red loam, well mixed. The soil will hide the cords, and it may be topped with a layer of pleasing green mosses.

It is possible to prepare grooves and holes in flat stones by grinding them with emery and a fine copper pipe, but the many good adhesive resins on the market today make this laborous task obsolete.

One of the most important points in preparing these bonsai is packing adequate soil among the roots. Later, interesting undulations in the surface of the soil can be created to increase the effect of the tree.

Plants set on top of stones in a soil container and those planted on flat stones require frequent watering because their root soil is limited. Those set in a flat tray of water, however, may be treated as ordinary bonsai if a small amount of root soil is spread in the tray.

3 Effective Display

I. Planting

Bonsai please because they are expressions in miniature of natural trees. To achieve the best effect in small containers, good planting methods are of the greatest importance. For long ages, bonsai cultivators have studied to perfect this vital basic of the art, and we today must strive both to learn the old ways and to improve them if we can.

1. THE FRONT

The front of a bonsai, the part that is to be viewed, must show all the plant's best points at once, because after the container is in place it must not be moved.

Although expressed in words "finding the front" may sound simple, it is in fact so difficult that often a bonsai specialist cannot immediately decide. Briefly, however, the front should be the side which shows the entire tree from root spread to trunk and topmost point.

One need not be a cameraman or painter to tell which side of a tree in the forest shows the plant to best advantage; the same observing eye must be used in deciding which side of a bonsai is the front.

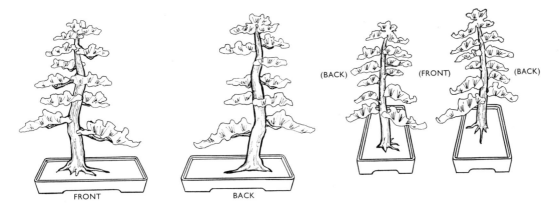

FRONT   BACK   (BACK)   (FRONT)   (BACK)

Fig. 36. Positioning. To determine front and back of a bonsai, examine these features: (1) root spread; (2) condition of trunk from roots upward; (3) branch condition and direction.

77

When dealing with immature plants, examine the trunk first. Does it rise straight; does it become slender naturally toward the top? Next cut off any innecessary branches, and re-examine the tree to determine the front side. Plant it so as to reveal the strongest root spread.

A mature planted tree always occupies the position in its container that the original cultivator selected as the front, but when replanting, examine it closely to see whether some other position might reveal its best points more interestingly. If a new angle from which the alternating branches and the shape of the tree seems lovelier catches your eye, use it. But if nothing novel occurs to you, return the tree to its previous position.

Finally, in selecting the front, do not become totally absorbed in the shape alone. Remember that a tree has an inward dignity that must be appropriately displayed.

2. POSITION AND ANGLE

After selecting the front side, you must determine the best position in the container. Before planting, select a pot of suitable size. One that is too small will not only force the branches to jut too far beyond the edges, but will also result in a cramped, unpleasant mood, whereas one that is too large will destroy the unity and compactness of the composition. For trees with thick trunks, choose a deep pot, and for those with slender trunks or for connected-roots bonsai, use shallow ones. Naturally, cascade bonsai require deep containers.

To determine position, examine the plant from the front in relationship to the pot, and find the place at which compactness, suggestive qualities, spaciousness, and depth can be most thoroughly exploited.

In general, the base of the trunk should be on a line midway back from the front edge of the pot, but if the trunk leans forward or if the branches incline to the front, set the base farther back.

Avoid placing the trunk in the midpoint of the center line because this spot results in perfect right-left symmetry and a loss of life and interest.

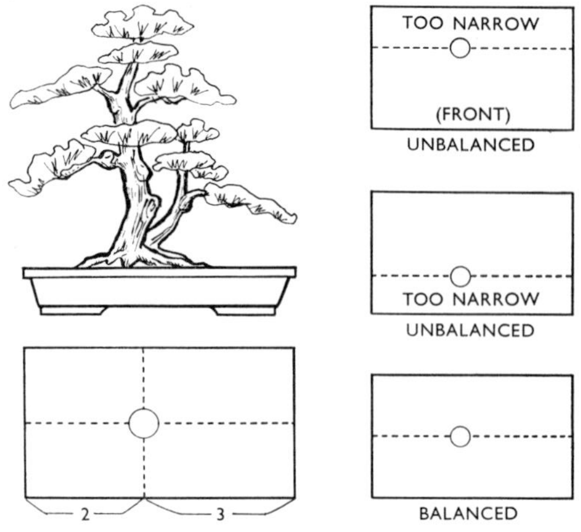

Fig. 37. Planting position. Branch projection determines right and left positioning, but the center line is best for front-back placement. Allow sixty per cent of the width of the pot to the side with the greatest branch projection.

Considering the center line to be composed of ten equal parts, place the trunk base so that three parts are on one side and seven on the other or so that four parts are on one side and six on the other. Whether the wider open area should be on the left or right depends on the shape of the tree: it must be on the side toward which the plant projects most.

The angle of planting, too, is determined by the shape of the tree: straight trees should be planted to point directly upward; curved or inclined ones must lean in the direction of their greater projection.

3. PLANTING THE VARIOUS BONSAI STYLES

A. Single Straight Trunk

The line from the base of the trunk to its tip must be perfectly straight. Balance must be maintained among the branches, their lengths and strengths, their directions and placements, and the distances among them. For the sake of depth, some should project to the sides of the container and some forward. Select the side from which the order of the branches appears to best advantage and from which branch spread is strongest. Roots should certainly spread well to right and left and, if possible, in all four directions. Straight-trunk bonsai must give the impression of being firmly rooted in the earth and of preserving total balance.

The rear side of a straight-trunk bonsai must meet the following conditions. It should lack the dignified rise of the front and should be weaker in feeling. The natural reduction in size of the trunk should be less apparent than on the front. By projecting to the rear, the branches on this side reduce the sense of depth, and when in full foliage conceal the trunk. Except in cases in which they spread in four directions, roots will be inconspicuous in the rear; therefore, the tree will resemble a stick thrust into the ground. Rear branches that are directed frontward, those that grow as high as one third the way from the tip of the plant, and short branches that put out leaves seemingly directly from the trunk may be left untouched because they do not conceal the trunk and, in fact, contribute to the beauty of the bonsai.

Correct slightly curving trunks with wire before planting.

Rounded-oval or rectangular pots are best for straight-trunk bonsai, and pines and evergreen oaks look more elegant in pots of reddish or purplish gray. Finally, for trees with thick trunks, select deep containers.

B. Slanting Trunk

To create maximum balance, stability, beauty, and depth with slanting-trunk bonsai, the front must be the side at which the tree leans forward to display its tip. Consequently, the rear may show a poor trunk line, will be excessively leafy, and will lack balance among trunk, branches, and root base.

After having selected the front, plant the tree so that the widest open space in the container is on the side of the incline of the trunk. Ideally, the greatest

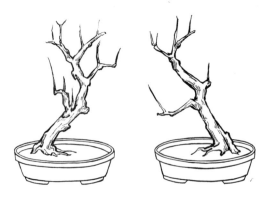

Fig. 38. Positioning slanted and elaborately bent trees. Though extreme cases are sometimes difficult to judge, by and large, the slant of the trunk determines the direction of movement of the total tree form. Allow most space for the side toward which the tree slants; in cases of strong double bends, the proportions may be relaxed.

root projection should be on this side too. For instance, if the tree inclines to the right, it should be set on the center line between front and back and far enough to the left so that two-thirds of the container's width are open on the right side. Obviously, the reverse is true for trees that lean to the left.

Select the position for the tree on the basis of the incline of the trunk only; the incline and projection of the branches are insignificant. Shallow containers, either rounded ovals or rectangles, are best.

C. Double Trunk

Since both the major trunk and the subordinate trunk, which reinforces it, must be shown to good advantage, select as front the side where both rise well and where the root spread is good. The major trunk must be straight to prevent serious loss of tone and dignity.

Should the two trunks lean in separate directions, select as front the side from which the major trunk inclines forward for depth and from which the incline of the subordinate trunk is appealing. The front must also show the best distance between the two trunks, harmonious trunk lines, and a root spread suggesting stability.

Because, in ideal double-trunk bonsai, the main trunk is straight, follow the same placement procedures as for straight-trunk trees: think of the width of the container as consisting of ten parts and set the plant to leave three parts on one side and seven on the other or four parts on one side and six on the other. The tree must be planted on the mid-line between the front and back of the container. Whether the subordinate trunk inclines to the left or right of the main trunk determines whether the wider open space is on the right or left side of the pot.

Rounded oval or rectangular shallow containers harmonize well with these trees.

D. Bent Trunk

The front of these bonsai must be the side from which the curves in the trunk appear most handsome and from which the root spread looks best. It must also show maximum branch projection. Often, determining the direction is difficult from examination of the bends alone, but it can be easily decided by simply turning the tree in the direction of the inclination of the tip of its trunk.

When the curves in the branches and trunk are moderate, place the tree in the pot as you would a straight-trunk plant (on the center line, three or four parts of the width of the container on one side and seven or six on the other).

When the curves are extreme, however, you may have to place the tree on the center line or farther to the back of the pot depending on the extent to which the trunk and branches lean forward. Furthermore, to create a sense of depth, it is sometimes necessary to plant the tree so that the trunk and branches incline.

Should the trunk lean backward, strict balance must be maintained among the largest low branch, the largest rear-projecting branch, the branches thrusting outward right and left, the root spread, and the curves of the total form.

Shallow oval pots suit curved-trunk trees, though, if the trunk is thick, a deeper container may be needed.

E.   Root-clump Groups

For best effect, these plants must be set with the side exhibiting the straightest, strongest aspect of the main trunk and the most stable root base turned forward. Ideally, if the major trunk is straight all the others must be also; if the major curves, so must the others. All the subordinate trunks must lean in the same direction as the major one. For placement purposes, consider the whole group one tree, and set them to maintain good separation from all viewpoints.

As a rule, the group should be set on the center line between the front and back of the container, but the nature of the inclination of trunk and branches may make slight alterations necessary. The trunks must never appear to block one another, and the total mood should be that of a grove or forest.

Bear in mind the frequent need to correct the rise of the trunks and the distances among them after the plant is in the container.

F.   Group Planting

Select as front the side that gives a feeling of depth: the small trees must be in the back and the single main trunk in the foreground. The front must show the main tree as a distinct entity, must reveal no overlapping trunks from any vantage point, and must be compact and harmoniously unified.

The main plant, which must stand on the center line between front and back of the pot and one third off center to right or left, should be tall and have a thick, stable trunk. To achieve the correct effect and to prevent any of the subordinate trees from being taller than the main one, it is necessary to prepare a group of twice as many trunks as will be needed in the finished bonsai. In addition, the number of trunks must always be an odd figure: three, five, seven, nine, eleven, etc.

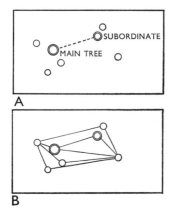

A

B

Fig. 39. Placement of group bonsai. (A) Even when viewd from an angle, no more than two trees should lie on the same straight line. (B) Arrange the trees to form scalene triangles from all vantage points.

To prevent the trunks from falling, wire them from the bottom of the pot. Take care, however, to see that the roots do not overlap to any great extent and that the trunks themselves do not crisscross each other. For the sake of stability and good root growth, pack plenty of soil among the roots.

G. Trees and Stones

Positioning for these bonsai depends largely on their three basic categories: plant and stone set in a container of water, plant and stone set in a pot of soil, plant for which the stone is the container.

Sometimes the tree is actually planted on the rock and sometimes its roots embrace the rock and pass into the soil below. In either case, the rocks are classified as tall or flat. Although tall-rock bonsai are more appealing to the eye, their technical difficulties make them unsuitable for beginner-cultivators. For reference, however, I might say that twisted-trunk and semi-cascade trees or those with far projecting branches lend themselves best to the style. On the other hand, for the less attractive, but simpler, flat-rock style, connected-roots or group-planting trees are best.

Bonsai set directly on flat stones without convential containers produce an effect of limitless space that is impossible with pots; connected-roots plants are most suitable.

The front of a stone and plant bonsai must be the side on which the lines of the tree blend with those of the rock. It must be completely stable, and the plant must be set so that neither its branches nor its roots conceal the good points of the stone. In brief, compensate for shortcomings in the tree branches by use of the stone and for those in the stone by use of the tree.

Finally, carefully match the tree to the mood of the stone: pines with rocks that suggest islands, cryptomeria cedars with those evoking images of valleys and ravines, maples with stones that resemble waterfalls.

H. Connected Roots

Since, in contrast to the frankly artificial raft-style, these bonsai strive for a natural mood by employing trees that in the wild crawl along the ground

Fig. 40. Flawed plants successfully used as bonsai with stones. (A) Create a lakeside feeling by lowering either the right or the left side of a tree with a U bend. (B) Trees bent this way are attractive leaning in the same direction as the lines of the stone on which they stand. (C) Suggest an ancient pine on a boulder by concealing the unstable part of the trunk. Stripping the bark (*jin*) from one of the upper branches directs attention there.

(silver spruce, five-needle pine, azalea, Japanese quince, etc.), any man-made element in their appearance reduces their aesthetic value.

Planting should be designed to take full advantage of the balanced lengths and sizes of trunks springing from a branch that has fallen to the ground. Perhaps the single-line placement viewed from the side results in a loss of depth, but to complain of this would be to ignore the value of having reproduced a condition that occurs in nature. Some connected-roots bonsai are natural, and some are man-made. The latter are the result of forcing a branch to rise straight up at a point one-third along another branch lying on the ground.

In spite of some formal difficulties, if, after artificially forcing this growth, you leave the rest to nature, in a few years the man-made tree will be so like one created in the forest that distinguishing between them will be impossible.

I. Cascade

Select the side from which the root base seems most secure and from which the cascading branch appears to best advantage as the front.

The nature of the pots used for cascades—deep and either square or nearly square—determines the placement of the plant. Balance between the cascading branch or trunk and the upper section is of the greatest importance, but in general, the tree should be set on or near the center point of the pot. Special care is required when the root spread of the tree is unidirectional.

In addition, if you ignore taking into consideration the height of the pedestal on which the tree will rest, you run the risk of destroying the distinctive, mystic dignity of this style.

Trees in which the upper and the cascading sections balance are ordinary cascades: those in which the cascading branches are larger than the upper ones called great cascades.

Be very carefull to avoid damaging the trunks and branches of these trees. Furthermore, since trees of this style are usually completely formed before final potting, once they are in the container, do not attempt to forcibly alter their shapes. Avoid putting them near large containers of water or in places where rain can splash mud on their lower branches.

J. Semi-cascade

Since they do not dip as deeply as cascades, these trees usually have tips pointed straight up. The trunk inclines slightly, and the branches curve gradually downward midway their lengths. In general, the degree of downward movement is less than half that of a full cascade. Consequently, positioning must take advantage of both the inclined trunk and the dipping branches.

In determining the front, take into consideration the requirements of both tree types. In other words, though it is important to utilize the downward slant of the cascade, you must also contrive to give expression to the upward striving of the leaves in their search for sunlight. Ideally, one large upward directed branch should offset the downward movement.

Emphasis should always be on the cascading bent trunk and branches. The placement in the pot must be determined by these two elements, the shape of the pot, and the roots spread; pay special attention to trees whose roots spread in one direction only.

II.   Trunk and Branches to Best Advantage

Unfortunately, few of the trees brought from fields and mountains make good bonsai as they are; most of them have several faults. But, with a little brain work, it is frequently possible to create striking arrangements by combining plants that lack sufficient appeal to be potted alone or by using apparently worthless plants together with suitable stones.

Some slanting-trunk trees that are unsightly alone become quite handsome when planted in twos so that the inclination of one balances that of the other. Three trees—one large, one medium, and one small—whose elevations are excessive and unattractive take on new beauty when planted as a group.

It is a good idea to compensate for excessive root spread in pines, by planting such trees on top of stones. Maples with ugly U-shape bends at the root base can be inclined so that one leg of the U leans outward to right or left and then set on a stone to suggest a tree growing by a lake. Similarly, a plum with a sharp angular bend in the middle of the trunk can be inclined so that the base of the trunk and the section above the bend move in the same direction. Set on a stone, such trees become attractive bonsai. Black pines with trunks bent in such a way as to destroy the visual stability of the base can be set on stones to conceal their weakness. Further, by removing the bark from the upper branch and setting the tree on a stone it is possible to symbolize a pine growing on a rocky island in the sea.

There are many ways of combining and placing trees to compensate for their bad points, but it is also often advantageous to lay an ugly tree prone so that it ultimately develops into a connected-roots or a raft-style plant. Trees with long branches on one side only are especially well suited to this treatment.

III. Harmony between Bonsai and Container

The following are the generally accepted fundamental points to be observed in balancing plant and container, but since this is a matter of eye and sense of beauty, feel free to try other approaches as well as these. For instance, planting conifers in whitish and dark green could result in a novel and interesting mood.

1. POTS FOR CONIFERS

Subdued black, reddish, purplish or ivory grays and dark red are the best colors. For straight-trunk plants use rectangular pots with out-turned rims. For trees producing a soft feeling select ovals or squares and rectangles with rounded corners. Cascade trees do best in deep round or square containers.

Rectangular containers go well with more formal group plantings and oval ones with the gentler arrangements. Special ceramic plates or flat natural stones are suitable for creative designs.

2. DECIDUOUS TREES

Use deep rectangular or oval containers for thick-trunk trees and shallower ones for slender plants. Whitish, light green, and gray black containers are best with maples. Use containers with out-turned rims for thick-trunk imposing trees, and avoid pots of the same color as the leaves of the plant.

3. FLOWERING AND FRUIT-BEARING PLANTS

Gray or ivory rectangular pots match plum trees, but use shallow round, whitish, or light gray containers for trees in the literati style.

Black, purplish, bluish, or yellow pots are best with white flowering plants,whereas whitish and light gray containers match red flowers best. Since the positions on the plants of the flowers and fruits change each year, versatile round or multi-sided pots are better than rigid rectangular and oval ones.

4. GRASSES AND SMALL PLANTS

These containers should be as shallow as possible. Yellow and greenish brown are good.

IV. Caution in Displaying

1. CHANGES IN DISPLAY STYLES

Until the end of the first quarter of this century, bonsai, almost always displayed in complicated arrangement in the ornamental alcoves (*tokonoma*) of formal rooms or tearooms, were frequently accompanied by calligraphy scrolls, incense burners, trays of fruits, or other objects, Buddhist statues, tea-ceremony implements, pedestals, small tables or screens. Although the same kind of display continued to be popular for many years, changes in daily life and in architectural styles gradually worked alterations in attitudes toward bonsai. Instead of the property of the privileged, they tended to become more generally popular, and after about 1935, principles for displaying them began to change.

The first major change was the tendency to isolate bonsai from other art objects and to display them for their own beauty alone. Instead of a subordinate role, the bonsai came to be the principle feature of the ornamental alcove and, as such, was most often accompanied by only grasses or attractive polished stones. Even when scrolls were used, their primary purpose was to emphasize the natural beauty of the plant. Consequently, realistically drawn pictures of trees were avoided in favor of views of mountains and rivers because the former detract from and the latter enhance the effect of the bonsai. The fact is, however, that calligraphy scrolls lend themselves to bonsai better than scrolls with pictures. Furthermore, screens with pictures and texts are best avoided in favor of unpatterned ones.

The second major change in bonsai display practices involves an increasing tendency to groups of one, two, or three bonsai unaccompanied by any other objects. The older elaborate exhibition, with its blue carpet, gold screen, calligraphy scrolls, incense burners, and tea-ceremony implements, gave way to the simpler, more efficient group of tables of proper heights placed before a white or cream background and ornamented with bonsai alone.

Finally, the restrictions on places in which the bonsai may acceptably be displayed have vanished. In former times, only the tokonoma or the front of a small screen were considered proper settings, but now bonsai brighten the entranceway, the sitting room, corridors in reinforced concrete buildings, and even kitchens. The only point demanding caution is careful balance among the size of the bonsai, the height of the table or platform it rests on, and the space around it. Today, bonsai are predominantly small or moderate in size, though large evergreens appear in exhibitions and are effectively displayed in the entrance lobbies of big buildings.

Finally, bonsai should be placed as near eye level as possible.

2.   SEASONS FOR DISPLAY

Each type of bonsai has its own optimum display season. Although most of the evergreens change little during the year, the silver spruce is handsome in April and May when its new buds appear. The Chinese junipers, too, are best in those months and tend to lose some of their loveliness in July and August. The five-needle pine is not at its best in the autumn when its old leaves turn brown. Elms and birches are beautiful in March and April when their new buds first appear, but stripped of leaves for winter, they are also lovely in a different way, especially if they have a dense growth of small, thin, soft branches.

Maples, of course, are gorgeous when their new buds have just appeared and in the autumn when their leaves turn gold, but they are also graceful and appealing when all their leaves have fallen.

Naturally, flowering and fruit-bearing trees should be shown when at their peaks: for plum, winter-flowering yellow jasmine, and Japanese quince January and February are best. Willows and tamarisk are most beautiful in the early summer after all of their leaves are out.

In Japan, pines and evergreens—especially the black pine and the five-needle pine—are widely used for New Year decoration and ornaments on other congratulatory occasions.

3.   SETTING

From the viewpoint of the health of the plant, always provide good lighting and ventilation to avoid breaking of the leaves and general loss of stamina. Ventilation is extremely important in the summer when stagnant air results in steaming and conditions injurious to plant physiology. Avoid keeping bonsai in heated rooms, and except in the dead of winter, put them out-of-doors every night to allow the dew to drench them. If you can meet all these requirements, the only other placement problem of importance is background and balance with the table on which the bonsai stands.

4.   PLACEMENT AND BALANCE WITH TABLE

Always display the tree to take best advantage of its good features because to ignore the accents that create the individual character of each plant is to greatly diminish the bonsai's aesthetic value.

Platforms for displaying bonsai may be tall, medium, or short and may be made of a variety of materials: rosewood, ebony, ironwood, boxwood, speckled bamboo (*Phyllostachys migra Munro*), etc. In addition, instead of a formal table, platforms are sometimes pieces of tree trunk in natural shapes.

In determining proper heights for the elements in a bonsai display, keep effective accent in mind. For instance, place a semi-cascade, five-needle pine bonsai on a moderately tall piece of tree trunk, and constrast it with a stone set on a low flat table or in a shallow tray filled with soil. Placed on the same height, the tree and the stone would be uninteresting, whereas separated by too great a height difference they would fail to balance. When the bonsai and its accompanying object must be on the same general level, create small height variations by means of pedestals and low platforms. Ornamental stones are often set on platforms, in shallow trays of soil, or on mats made of bamboo slats.

Small bonsai look best on simple ornamental shelves. If a group of them is simply aligned on one level, their smallness makes the arrangement seem cluttered. On the other hand, set on large, decorative shelves, they are over-shadowed.

A final word of caution, never pull a bonsai pot across the surface of a fine wooden platform or table. No matter how excellent the materials of which the table is made, unsightly scratches on its top make it worthless for ornamental purposes.

5. PLACEMENT OF THE POT AND THE ACCOMPANYING OBJECTS

When displaying more than two bonsai in the same arrangement, you must balance them carefully. Although unglazed pots are the most commonly used for conifers, they are not the only kinds. The range of pottery colors includes whitish, gray black, and light blue; and shapes may be rectangular, oval, round, square, or flower-formed. For best effect, combine different shapes and colors to produce interesting contrasts. For instance, combine a black pine potted in a reddish, unglazed rectangular container with an ar-rangement of grasses in a whitish oval pot. In short, avoid monotony and dullness by never using more than one pot of the same color and shape.

To conclude my remarks on placement, I should like to emphasize again the importance of variety to a truly outstanding bonsai display. On the other hand, though height and shape variations are essential, the whole composi-tion must maintain harmonious balance. This is best achieved by con-trasting accompanying objects with the main element of the design, in this case, the bonsai itself. Use any number of accompanying objects that you think necessary, but remember that they must all have appeal of their own and the softness of one must be used to contrast with the rigid qualities of the other. For instance, deciduous trees, stones with a gentle appearance, or grass bonsai effectively balance formal conifers.

Seeds for the five-needle pine (right) and the maple (left). Many bonsai plants are grown directly from just such seeds.

Preparations

Seed

1.   Chinese quince (two years old, ten inches high) grown from seeds.
2.   For transplanting, the Chinese quince has been removed from the pot (right) and has had its roots trimmed (left).
3.   The same Chinese quince after transplantation (right) and after the top has been trimmed (left) to force the development of lateral branching, essential to bonsai cultivation.
4.   Lateral branching resulting from trimming the top of the plant (seven years old).

1   2

4   3

89

Cuttings

Cuttings (second year, one inch high) from an adult silver spruce.

1   2

1. Discarded branches from a full-grown cryptomeria cedar used as cuttings (one year, five inches high).

2. (right) A cryptomeria cedar cutting one year after planting. (left) The same cutting after its roots have been trimmed.

3. The cryptomeria cedar cutting after potting.

3

1. Branches pruned from azaleas (*Rhododendron kiusianum*) and potted as cuttings: (left) one year, (right) two years and from four to five inches in height.

2. A two-year plant removed from the pot (right) has its roots trimmed (left).

3. At two years, roots reach these lengths.

4. Potted two-year plants.

Cuttings

Selected pruned cuttings from camellias approximately three months after planting.

Root Divisions

1. This buttercup winterhazel (five years, one foot and six inches) will be divided in the middle and repotted.
2. This yellow azalea (*Rhododendron japonicum*—five years, one foot and six inches) must be divided in the middle and transplanted.

Layering

Black pine. The trunk must be shortened for the sake of the beauty of the shape.

Pruning

Pruning a Chinese quince. Although the procedure varies with the shape of the tree, it is customary to leave two or three leaves on the small branches.

Pruning maples. Cut halfway up the petiole.

Cut away about two-thirds of zelkova branches.

After pruning.

▽

Pruning

1. A ten-year old, cutting-grown azalea (*Rhododendron lateritium*) after blooms have fallen. (below) Although the azalea above looks stark after pruning, in a year the foliage will reach excessive luxuriance again.

OPPOSITE PAGE:

2. A ten-year old azalea (*Rhododendron lateritium*), before (above) and after (below) pruning.

3. A ten-year old seed-grown zelkova before (above) and immediately after pruning and bud plucking (below). Since it will produce too many leaves in only thirty or forty days, this plant requires trimming three or four times a year.

2

▽

▽

4. A well cared for two-year old (fifteen inches high) cryptomeria cedar before (upper) and after (lower) pruning.

5. Two-year old cryptomeria cedars being trained to become a connected-roots style bonsai (upper). The lower picture shows the same cedars after pruning.

6.   A tamarisk (*Tamarix chinensis*) cutting six months after planting. At right is the same tamarisk after wiring.

7.   Another six-month tamarisk cutting before (below left) and after wiring (below right).

1. A ten-year old *Pyracantha augustifolia* raised from a cutting. Its branches have spread well, and its trunk is thick.

2. First prune and shape the plant.

3 4

3. Next, match the plant to the new pot, by marking its width on the root mass with sticks; and taking care not to damage or cut the roots more than necessary, unpack the plant.

4. Trimming the roots.

6 7

5. After trimming the roots on the left and right, cut those in front and back. The sticks in the root mass mark the width of the new pot (left).

6. Spread small pieces of plastic screen over the drainage holes, and pass pieces of twine through them to hold the plant in place.

7. Spread coarse gravel over the bottom.

8. Sprinkle moderate soil on top of the gravel.

8

9

10

→

12

9. Put the plant in place, and secure it with twine.

10. Sprinkle soil lightly around the plant.

11. Eliminate openings among the soil particles with a slender stick—in this case bamboo chopsticks—and add more soil.

12. Tap the sides of the pot lightly with the fist to pack the soil in the peripheral area.

13. Level the soil surface with a trowel.

14. View from the side. The left is the front of the bonsai.

15. After finishing with a top layer of fine soil, douse with water till it flows out of the drainage holes in the bottom.

14

11

13

15

1

2

Jin, Sabamiki, and Uro

1. Five-needle pine with a whitened branch (*jin*) and a whitened section of trunk (*sabamiki*).

2. The hollowed-out section in this five-needle pine is called *uro*.

3. Another five-needle pine with whitened branch and trunk section.

4. A five-needle pine with a *sabamiki* on a low section of the trunk.

Distinctive Trunk Shapes and Bonsai with Stones

3

4

Bonsai with Stones

Twine used to hold the bonsai plant in place on the stone must be fixed securely in the stone grooves with V-shaped lead wedges. (below) Azaleas (*Rhododendron japonicum*) planted in dry moss, red loam, sand, and held in place with twine, are complemented by a layer of green mosses planted around them.

Fixing the twine in place with lead wedges.

To secure the twine, it is best to use a stone with plenty of grooves and cracks. (below) The stone at right now ornamented with a silver spruce bonsai.

A ten-year old silver spruce bonsai planted on a stone.

A one-year old black pine bonsai on a stone.

Harmonizing the Plant and the Pot

1. Quiet, deciduous trees look best in shallow oval trays. Plant: maple; container: oval, light blue tray.

2. Conifers that give an impression of strength should be planted in moderately deep, rectangular containers. Plant: black pine; container: reddish, unglazed rectangular pot.

3. Deep round pots are best with cascade and semi-cascade bonsai. Plant: black pine; container: reddish, unglazed round pot.

Displaying Bonsai

1. A miscanthus (*Miscanthus sinensis*) bonsai combined with a rock symbolizing a bird suggests the waterside. Bonsai displays must create a unified whole. (This arrangement is set on a bamboo mat.)

2. Japanese cypress in the main pot and grasses in the minor one evoke the mood of the fields. The base for the grass bonsai contrasts pleasing with the more formal platform for the cypress.

1

2

3. Bonsai with an ornamental stone. The effect of a literati-style black pine with a range of mountains in the distance.

4. A group of small bonsai. Arrangements of this kind must strive for unity of mood. The materials (left to right) are grasses (lower), black pine (upper), maple, Japanese quince and juniper. Rhythm is developed in the total display by means of the following placements.

(1) The major lines of all the bonsai on the left move to the left.

(2) The long branch of the small Japanese quince moves sharply right.

(3) The juniper, rising straight upward, stops the movement flow.

Tools

All that is necessary for wiring a bonsai.

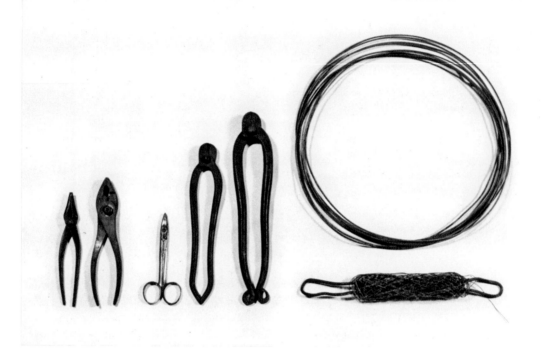

Equipment for planting. Sifters (far right)
come in three or four grades of coarseness.

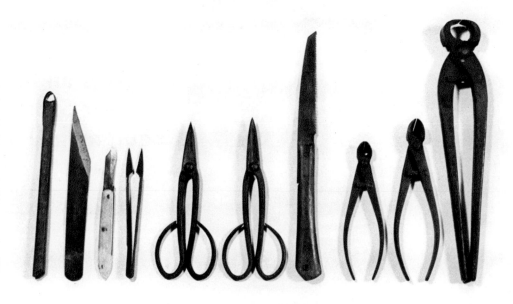

Tools for pruning, shaping branches, and forming bonsai. The implement on the far left is for stripping bark, that on the far right is used to cut off knots.

Watering equipment. It is a good idea to attach the nozzle from a sprinkling can to the end of a hose.

Though more time consuming, simple use of the sprinkling can itself is standard.

Cultivation Shelves and Winter Storing Equipments

Bonsai shelves, thick boards on stone supports. At a height of about two feet, the shelves are convenient for working with and admiring the plants. They should be in sunny places.

(Left) Winter storage. Trees that can endure the cold may be set outdoors under the eaves of a building.

(Upper) Weaker plants must be kept indoors in the winter, but they should always be set outdoors in the daytime to get plenty of sunlight.

4 Care

I. Soil and Repotting

1. SOIL

In some instances bonsai soil is primarily loam, and in others largely sand. Sand requires more frequent watering and great care to preserve a moisture level during dry seasons, and though it absorbs fertilizer nutrients quickly, it does not store them well and, therefore, does not build endurance in the plant. Consequently, the current trend is away from sand in favor of loamy soils. Some plants prefer sand, and often it is good to blend soils to recreate as closely as possible the natural conditions of the individual plant. By and large, however, the main considerations in preparing bonsai soils are adequate water retention and good ventilation. The sandiest soils used are those containing either seven parts sand to three of earth or half sand and half earth. Soil mixtures containing less sand require less frequent watering.

The main types of soil for bonsai cultivation are black loam, red loam, light gravelly soil, soil mixed with compost, river sand, and mountain sand. The black loam found near the surface in gardens and agricultural fields is both too fine grained and too poorly fertilized; consequently, it is best to take soil from about one or two feet below the surface of the ground and to spread it on the surface to dry for a week or two. Later, using sifters of one-quarter, one-eighth, and three-eighths inches, separate the soil into three grades. Do not use anything finer than a one-eighth-inch grain. The same sifting procedure and grading applies to all bonsai soils.

Deriving its color from the large amount of iron oxide it contains, red loam should also be dug from about one or two feet below the surface of the ground and treated just as black loam.

Consisting of lumps of light gravel—pumice—about one-eight of an inch in diameter, gravelly soil is either gray or reddish brown and has a much greater water retention capacity than other soils. Furthermore, since the spaces among its particles are large, it allows extremely good ventilation.

Because it contains large quantities of decaying leaves and small branches and is, therefore, both rich and porous, compost not only nourishes plants, it also assists in ventilating them.

Sea sand is both too fine and too heavily salt laden to be of bonsai use.

113

Sand from the upper reaches of streams drains well but retains little water; consequently, it is less suitable for watering and fertilizing than mountain sand.

Composed of both pumic and lava, mountain sand absorbs water because of the properties of the former and holds water for long time on the rough surface of latter. Furthermore, since it also drains well, it is superior to river sand for bonsai purposes.

Soil and sand percentage standards for various trees are as follows: pines—five parts sand, four parts red loam, one part black loam; other evergreens—three parts sand, five parts red loam, two parts black loam; flowering and fruit-bearing trees—three parts sand, five parts red loam, one part black loam, and one or two parts soil mixed with compost. These ratios vary in accordance with fertilizing practices during cultivation.

Combinations of different coarse, lumpy soils, by increasing water retention and, consequently, providing for both plants that absorb nutrients quickly and those that require more time, make it possible to repot at wider intervals.

Repotting is a surgical operation that reduces the number of active roots left to a plant and should, therefore, be performed only when cultivation soil has lost the majority of its nourishing elements. Always care for plants and use good mixed soils in potting so that the following average interval between replantings can be maintained: conifers, five or six years; other evergreens and many deciduous trees, three or four years; flowering and fruit-bearing bonsai, two or three years. Although, at present, repotting compensates for insufficiencies in fertilizers and care inadequacies, future research, particularly in the prevention of fertilizer oxidation, may reduce the necessary frequency of replantings.

Some plants prefer the soil conditions prevalent in the mountains, others those of the beaches or fields. The following list should be helpful in guiding your preparations for potting most plants. Bear in mind these two points, however, no matter what kind of tree you are cultivating. 1. Use only fresh, germ-free materials. 2. Pines thrive in sandy soil, and flowering or fruit-bearing plants as well as all fast growing trees do better in soils that are a mixture of three to six parts sand and clayey earth or in those that have an admixture of organic matter.

Pines

Pines producing numerous needles from single buds require more sand; those with single needles, less.
1.   Mountain sand or river sand, six parts; red loam, four parts.
2.   Mountain or river sand, five parts; red loam, one part; black loam, one part.
3.   Mountain or river sand, three parts; red loam, four parts; black loam, four parts.

Evergreen Oaks and Cryptomeria Cedars

1. Mountain or river sand, five parts; red loam, five parts.
2. Mountain or river sand, four parts; red loam, four parts; black loam, two parts.

Other Evergreens and Deciduous Trees

1. Mountain or river sand, four parts; red loam, four parts; black loam, two parts.
2. Mountain or river sand, three parts; red loam, five parts; black loam, two parts.

Flowering or Fruit-Bearing Plants

Mountain or river sand, three parts; red loam, four parts; black loam, three parts.
(Since the flowering and fruit-bearing plants require ample fertilizer, reduce the amount of sand in their mixture in favor of soils that retain water and promote rapid root growth.)

2. REPOTTING

Today, fertilizers make it possible to adjust soil conditions during cultivation; nonetheless, you must always watch for lime deficiencies. Plants have a low acid tolerance and thrive best in neutral soil. To lighten your repotting labor and to improve the plant's water intake, always use eighty per cent dried, germ-free soil in transplanting; generally repot in spring or autumn at approximately the vernal or autumnal equinox.

A certain amount of accuracy is needed in order to repot a tree so that it remains in the position that displays its shape to best advantage and to prevent possible loss of the plant. Of course, it is sometimes possible to improve the appearance of the bonsai by altering its position during repotting.

I will use the pine as an example in explaining the repotting procedure, but remember that these trees will not tolerate total removal of old soil. Some must be left among the roots for protection.

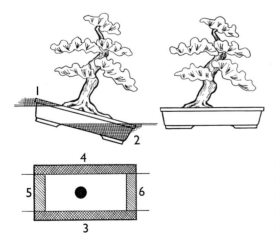

Fig. 41. To alter the position of a tree during replanting, place the old pot so that the tree is in the desired new posture, remove it from the pot, and cut the roots and remove the soil accordingly. In other words, in the illustrated tree, it is necessary to remove the soil in shaded areas 1 and 2. If you do not intend to alter the slant of the tree, removing the soil in 1 is unnecessary.

Before removing the soil and cutting the roots, ascertain the size and depth of the new pot and the position the tree will have when repotted. If the slant of the tree is to be altered, first shave the surface soil so that it will be horizontal in its new position. This is unnecessary, of course, if the posture of the plant is to remain unchanged. Remove small amounts of soil at a time to avoid damaging the roots themselves. Next remove enough soil from the bottom of the root mass to suit it to the depth of the new pot and to insure the tree's standing in the proper posture. After having done this, remove enough soil from the front and back of the mass to facilitate packing in the new soil; and then, after establishing the lateral position of the plant in the pot, remove a similar amount of soil from the right and left sides of the mass. In doing so, bear in mind the placement rules for the various tree styles (see Chapter Three, page 77).

Removing soil from small bonsai can be done without measuring: but when working with larger trees, use a ruler to mark off the correct amounts of soil to be taken away, and designate the correct spots with small sticks. In this way you can safely produce the desired effect without either cutting off too many roots or making measurement mistakes. Be especially careful to follow proper procedures when working with superior bonsai.

In moving, or sometimes because of strong winds, bonsai can be accidentally pulled from the pot. Prevent this by fixing the tree securely with ropes passed through the drainage hole in the pot bottom. This is doubly essential because, even when the danger of accidental toppling does not exist, an insecurely fixed tree will not grow properly; and after repotting, its roots will not recover as quickly as they should. Although copper wires were formerly used in fixing plants in place, today covered wire or hemp rope is preferred.

Repotting involves cutting the active plant root ends, but since these are vital to life, limits must be set on the amount the plant can safely do without. The maximum amount permissible to remove is two-thirds of the total, and the usual is one-half. Though pines will not tolerate severe root cutting, deciduous trees, whose active root ends grow quite long, should be cut back until the root-soil mass will comfortably fit into the new pot. Repot pines in spring and fall around the equinoxes, but plants from southern regions should not be repotted until after the vernal equinox or during the rainy summer weather (in Japan, June and July). Recent cultivation

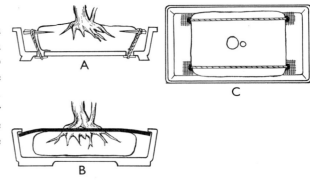

Fig. 42. Three methods for fixing a tree in place after transplanting. (A) Insert wooden pegs into the soil, attach loops of twine to them, run the loops through the drainage holes, and fix them in place with small sticks. (B) Insert two slender sticks under the inner ridges of the pot in front and back. (C) Tie the tree in place with ropes run through the drainage holes.

theories hold that autumn replanting should be done in mid- or late August or early or mid-September. Repot, prune, and wire cryptomeria cedars and Japanese cypress *only* well after the vernal equinox, but deciduous trees that will stand pruning in June or July, may be repotted at the same time.

A very recent technique calls for repotting old bonsai after the new buds are out and firmly fixed, but unless thorough study accompanies this approach, it is dangerous to the life of the plant.

Because the active roots of bonsai that have not been repotted for more than five or six years will probably be dead, do not repot in the orthodox way. First, without cutting any of the roots, transfer the plant to a larger pot. After it has stood for six months to one year and has generated new active root ends, repot in the ordinary fashion. Old bonsai are valuable and deserve the best care to eliminate the possibility of their being thoughtlessly destroyed.

Azaleas—both *Rhododendron indicum* and *Rhododendron lateritium*—should be repotted either in the early spring or during the wet weather in early summer after the flowers have bloomed and the plant has been pruned. Although specialists who concentrate on raising azaleas only and take their plants from the mountains employ a cultivation soil containing two or three parts shpagnum moss, gravelly pumice soil is more common.

Repot flowering and fruit-bearing bonsai, which bloom largely in the spring, either after the flowers have fallen or in the autumn.

II. Plant Diseases and Their Treatment

1. DISEASES

Well cared for plants rarely fall victim to sickness, and even when they do, cure is easy. Trees subjected to careless or inadequate treatment for long periods, on the other hand, frequently wither; seedlings and young plants may suddenly dry up and die or branches of older trees dry and turn brown with no apparent cause. Although bacteria are sometimes the villain, in general the ultimate source of the trouble is poor soil, lack of repotting, or insufficient fertilizing. Symptoms occur most often in seasons of high heat and humidity. The best cure is a watchful eye that catches the sickness at the earliest stage when organic mercurial chloride may be used to eradicate the difficulty.

Conifers are susceptible to plant rust, an aggregation on the branches or trunk of parasitic basidia resembling reddish or brownish iron oxide. These pests reproduce by cell division and can extend over considerable areas in a week or ten days. To destroy them repeated applications of lime sulfur are necessary.

The white powdery cells that infect azaleas, camellias, and maples and cause swellings in the diseased area, usually go unnoticed because the harm they do is inconspicuous; nevertheless, their cause is bacteria that may be destroyed by the use of insecticides containing copper.

Although many diseases are caused by bacteria, fertilizers play an important role in limiting the extent of their spread: nitrogen fertilizers alone make plants susceptible to disease; wheres potassic manures tend to supress their growth. Consequently, careful blending of fertilizing materials is essential.

Sometimes a narrowly limited disease can be cured by cutting off the sick part, but since bonsai are usually carefully shaped and each branch is important, insecticides and chemicals are preferable.

Be sure to match the chemical to the disease. The most frequently used ones are Bordeaux mixture, and lime sulfur.

When sickness has progressed to the roots (a frequent occurrence with quince), at repotting time, remove all of the root soil, and disinfect with a suitable chemical. Pines, however, which will not tolerate the removal of all their root soil, should be especially carefully disinfected and treated with potassic fertilizer.

2. INSECT PESTS

Insecticides will usually take care of conspicuous pests, but to avoid the unsightly scars insects leave, it is important to take the precaution of spraying an agricultural chemical on all bonsai once every three weeks, from late spring through the summer and fall. BHC and DDT are most common, but they must be considerably thinned, especially when new buds are appearing, since plants, as well as insects, feel effects of chemicals.

Plant lice are so small that they are frequently overlooked and the signs of their presence—poor leaf color, loss of leaf luster, whitish leaves, and, in azaleas, reddish-brown leaves—are mistaken for illness or insufficient fertilizing. At the appearance of any of these symptoms, examine the plant carefully with a magnifying glass, and you may find countless small lice on the leaves or branches. The insects multiply rapidly, especially in hot, humid weather, and ordinary insecticides applied only once will not kill the eggs. For this reason, the plant should be sprayed three or four times at intervals of three or four days. Fortunately, however, certain recently developed insecticides destroy the eggs as well as the adult insects.

III. Fertilizing

The rapid exhaustion of nutrients in the limited amount of soil in a bonsai container necessitates frequent doses of fertilizer. In addition to the three major fertilizer elements many microscopic elements (calcium, iron, magnesium, potassium, phosphorous, and sulfur) may be added to promote optimum growth.

The following are the most widely used.
1. Nitrogen fertilizers
    rape-seed oil cake, soy-bean oil cake, dried and crushed small fish (ammonium chloride, lime nitrate, urea)

2. Potassic fertilizers
   vegetable ash, seaweed ash, (potassium sulphate, potassium chloride)
3. Phosphorous fertilizers
   bone meal, animal urea, rice husks (superphosphate)
4. Calcium fertilizers
   Raw lime, slaked lime (to neutralize soil acidity)

Customarily, equal quantities of rape-seed and soy-bean oil cakes, and fish meals mixed with water are kneaded into small loaves and placed at a few spots on the surface of the soil in the pot. As the plant is watered or as rain falls, the fertilizer dissolves and flows into the soil. However, in long periods of wet weather, over-fertilizing can result, and in droughts no fertilizing takes place at all. Furthermore, too much fertilizer can acidify the soil. Consequently, it is best to allow the fertilizer to ferment, grind it to a powder, and apply it in small quantites to the soil. Two or three times a year, vegetable ash disolved in water and poured on the soil will both fertilize and neutralize acidity.

To prepare a liquid fertilizer, dissolve one part of the solid matter in ten parts water to make a basic mixture. Further dilute this by adding one part of the basic mixture to ten parts water, and pour it on the soil once a week (three to four times a week in spring and autumn). Accompany this treatment with applications of some material to neutralize soil acid.

The described method is standard for ordinary cultivation, but for more special needs, the following method gives even greater results.

Because animal and vegetable material contains all the necessary elements plus important minor elements, bonsai cultivators generally do not use synthetic chemical fertilizers. Instead, they prepare their own mixtures in this way. In October or November, knead with water equal amounts of fish meal, soy-bean, and rape-seed oil cakes, and one-third that amount of rice husks. Shape the mixture into cakes, and wrap them in craft paper. Seal them tightly in a wooden box, put them in a shaded place, and allow them to stand undisturbed until July. Then, or even as late as August, expose them to strong sunlight, and, when they are dry, pulverize them. The powders will produce on effective fertilizer concentrate for all bonsai purposes. Convert the dry ingredient into a usable liquid fertilizer by thinning one part of the mix with 15,000 to 30,000 parts of water (a teaspoonful to four gallons of water), and sprinkle it on the plant. This method will give fast and excellent results, but remember that in certain seasons the fertilizer must be decreased and that in the case of certain plants requiring extra nourishment, the mixture should be increased to a strength of only 5,000 parts water to one of the concentrate.

Of the factors controlling the growth of plants—soil, watering, weather, and fertilizing—the last has probably been the subject of more serious study than any of the others, and since, like all living things, plants grow stronger and better with good daily nourishment, research on this topic will doubtless continue far into the future.

I have already mentioned the need to neutralize soil, but it is important to bear in mind the fact that soil must maintain a degree of acidity needed by the individual plant. Neutralizing is a basic bonsai procedure that must be repeated countless times. In the course of your bonsai experience, you will ultimately be able to determine how much neutralizing material is needed in a given instance by merely examining the soil with your eye. For the novice, however, litmus paper provides a reliable guide.

IV. Watering

Each plant needs certain amounts of moisture, and once the cultivator has learned to judge individual requirements, he can both produce maximum results and show his bonsai skill by proper watering.

The most reliable rule of thumb is that the majority of plants like rain, therefore watering, but cannot stand extended periods of wet weather, or excess humidity. Similarly, they need to be allowed to dry out but cannot tolerate droughts. Converted into easy-to-understand figures, this means that if we assign to the degree of water saturation reached just after sprinkling the value ten and zero to the point when all moisture has been exhausted, optimum conditions are those existing in the range between three and seven. Pines, however, should be kept a little dryer than other plants. Water more frequently on sunny days or when a dry wind is blowing. Naturally heavy drenchings, until water pours from the drainage hole in the bottom of the pot, extend the period between waterings.

The following watering times are standard, but certain adjustments may be necessary for individual plants.

In summer, water heavily three times a day—10:00 to 11:00 a.m.; 1:00 to 2:00 p.m. (wet the leaves to prevent scorching), and 4:00 to 5:00 p.m. In spring and fall, water twice a day—10:00 to 11:00 a.m.; 4:00 to 5:00 p.m. In winter water only once in the morning.

V. Storage and Seasonal Protection

Bonsai plants, prized for the changing seasonal beauty of their foliage and shapes, require the cultivator to adjust care according to the time of year. After all, roots, which should be growing free in the ground, are cramped in the limited confines of a small container. In short, because the natural growth of the plant is restricted to meet aesthetic needs, the cultivator must provide a good environment, no matter what the season.

To do this, he needs to understand the four major activities carried out by plants and the times when they take place. Plants grow in the spring, reach full fruition in the summer, prepare for cold weather in the autumn, and sleep during the winter.

To help a potted plant prepare for winter, first expose it two or three times to light autumn frost; then, choosing a sunny day, either bring it indoors or put it in some suitable protective shelter. Bonsai most in need of such

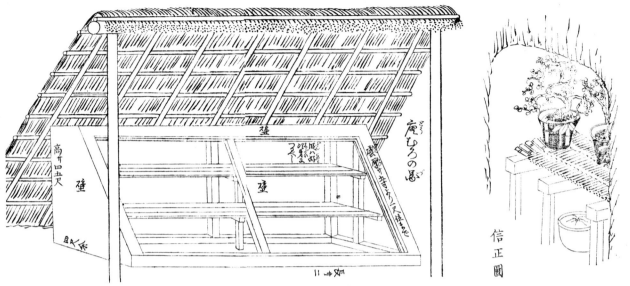

Fig. 43. A simple bonsai storage lean-to (from *Sōmoku Sodategusa*).

Fig. 44. Bonsai stored in a cave for winter (from *Sōmoku Sodategusa*).

protection are those from southern regions (pomegranates, mandarin oranges, etc.) and those in shallow or small containers.

In areas where the ground is frozen day and night for long periods, a cave-like excavation in a cliff-side, or shelter patterned on one, is needed. In regions where the ground freezes at night but thaws again in the morning, a roofed building with sufficient small openings for good ventilation provides the best protection. Plants that resist cold well may be kept out of doors, even though thin ice forms on the surface of the pot soil, as long as they do not come in direct contact with severe frost. Naturally, no protection is required in areas that do not experience night freezing. In severe winters, however, protective equipment is essential to prevent both pot breakage caused by freezing and destruction of the soil structure resulting from repeated night frosts and day thaws. Plants from southern zones are especially susceptible to cold damage.

Choose an early day in spring to remove the plants from their winter shelter to the open cultivation shelves, but be careful to avoid the last frosts of the year. When the greenery of the new growing season has appeared, it is time to repot and prune to improve or correct the shapes of bonsai. Plants that have not been repotted or wired may be removed to the outdoors earlier than those that have recently undergone such treatment; these latter require protection until the danger of late frosts has passed.

In early summer, all trees produce new buds and small branches. Until the new leaves are securely fixed on the branches, keep bonsai out of strong winds. This is also the time when insects cause greatest damage to leaves, but careful fertilizing will keep the pests under control.

A thoroughly treated bonsai, set in the bright sun and frequently watered, will require no special attention or protection during the summer months. On the other hand, imperfectly repotted trees or those with poor root conditions—for instance, trees only recently brought in from the mountains—demand a cool shady place. Furthermore, in areas where the summer sun is extremely hot and scorching, suitable protective steps must be taken.

Having reached full fruition and maximum strength, bonsai are at their best in the autumn, the season when they repay the cultivator for all of the attention he has expended on them. At this time, because they are using all their strength to prepare for their winter's sleep, trees should be fertilized one last time.

VI.   Reviving Bonsai in Poor Condition

1.   INSUFFICIENT SUNLIGHT

Although bonsai, largely plants from mountainous zones, prefer conditions similar to their natural environment, since they are considered objects of aesthetic appreciation and ornament, cultivators frequently keep them indoors under circumstances slightly different from those to which they are accustomed. As long as the artificial environment does not harm the tree, all is well; but extended stays indoors in heated rooms, even in winter, cause the spring buds to be pale and weak. On the other hand, sudden exposure to bright sunlight after a long time indoors, wilts the buds or desiccates and kills the new branches and leaves. The shift from dim surroundings to bright ones must be made gradually: from the indoors to a protective shelter or to a shady corner of the garden, and then into the bright sun.

2.   INSUFFICIENT VENTILATION

Trees require clean air to grow. Although demands differ with the kind of plant, generally, poor ventilation stunts growth and invites insect damage and sickness. Plants thrive in hot places, where ventilation is good, but in heat, humidity, and stagnant air, their life processes are paralyzed. As is true of returning plants to sunlight, however, the shift from a poorly ventilated place to a well ventilated one must be gradual.

3.   INSUFFICIENT WATERING

Drying, deadly to plants, is most likely to occur during the winter, while the plants sleep, or in early spring, their most vigorous growth period. Vertical cracks in the trunks and shriveled branches are symptoms of the condition, and steps must be taken to revive the plant before desiccation reaches these advance stages.

Trees that fail to produce new spring buds have either been stricken with cold or have lacked sufficient water during the winter. To cure this condition, the overturned bucket method is most effective. Bury pot and plant in the

Fig. 45. An inverted bucket used to protect a plant from the cold.

ground, and invert a bucket or similar container over it. Thus cut off from the outside air, the plant will gradually produce new buds, but it is essential to examine it from time to time and to water it to stimulate growth. Do not expose the plant to the outside air suddenly; instead gradually introduce ventilation until the tree is strong enough to return to its natural environment. The treatment should begin in late spring (in Japan, at the beginning of the rainy season). Remove the bucket when the tree has recovered, but select a rainy day for the plant's first exposure to the open air. This method works especially well on deciduous plants.

Needle-bearing trees, however, respond best to the following treatment. Place them in a protective shelter in which the temperature is moderate, reduce the amount of water given to the roots, and water the needles and branches heavily to increase humidity.

To treat for drying occuring from early spring to summer, water leaves, trunk, and pot soil heavily, and take precautions to insure that the water in the pot drains out quickly, because stagnant moisture will rot the roots and destroy the plant. If kept in a moderately well lighted, well ventilated place, and watered heavily on the leaves and moderately on the roots and soil, a plant suffering from a light case of drying will recover in a week. More severely desiccated plants require a protective shelter or special recuperative measures.

Prune the leaves of deciduous plants, and wrap the trunks and small branches of evergreen trees and evergreen oaks in sphagnum moss. Keep the afflicted plants in dimly lighted areas out of strong winds. Water the leaves and needles well, but restrict the amount of water poured around the roots, because when desiccation occurs, especially in evergreens, root hairs die, thus impairing the plant's water intake ability. Unless new root hairs are allowed to grow the plant will die, but too much water will cause root rot and total loss. Wrapping the trunk of the tree in moss and creating a condition of high humidity prevents further drying. Although ideal conditions can be maintained in a greenhouse, the treatment just prescribed is effective when such sophisticated facilities are unavailable. Care of the roots and prevention of rot is vital: water once well and then only moderately.

Damage caused by excess watering can be repaired by immediately returning the plant to standard treatment and by the application of a liquid fertilizer solution prepared from vegetable ash.

4. IMPROPER OR EXHAUSTED SOIL

Symptoms of improper and of exhausted soil are similar, but countermeasures used against them are slightly different. In the first instance, repotting is sufficient. In the second, repotting is sometimes suitable, but in other cases when excess trunk, branch, and leaf growth is undesirable, thorough fertilizing alone produces satisfactory results.

Soil that no longer ventilates or drains properly must be changed immediately.

5. EXCESS OR IMPROPER FERTILIZING

Though rare in winter, excess fertilizing often occurs from early spring to summer. Oil cake placed directly on the soil, ferments, and as it decomposes, acidifies the soil thus producing harmful bacteria. In slight cases, use a liquid solution of vegetable ash to neutralize the soil, keep the soil slightly dry, and place the plant in a dimly lighted, well ventilated place. Should the condition be more serious, after neutralizing the soil, repot; but care is necessary to avoid damaging the roots or shocking the plant.

6. SOILED PLANTS

Living organisms, plants must breathe to live, but the dirt, grime, soot, and smoke, of modern urban surroundings block their pores and age them faster than is desirable. The condition, however, is easily cured. First, water the leaves and trunks of bonsai daily to prevent the accumulation of grime. Should it get out of hand, however, grime can be washed away with a soft brush and a weak solution of neutral soap and water or with a thin, forceful stream of water.

7. INSECT DAMAGE

Insects multiply rapidly when the weather is warm and humid, but the many good insecticides on the market today will rid plants of the various pests to which they fall victim. The commonest insect villain, plant lice, however, requires either a special louse insecticide or repeated uses of ordinary insecticides to kill the insects hatching from the countless eggs laid on leaves and branches. Three or four applications of ordinary chemicals must be made at intervals of three or four days.

For best results, use the same insecticide at fixed intervals: about once every three or four weeks during the summer growing season. On the other hand, keeping a number of insecticide preparations on hand and using them alternately sometimes increases the effect of treatment.

8. SICKNESSES

Sickness indicates faulty care in either soil, ventilation, watering, sunlight, or fertilizing. Heavy reliance on nitrogen fertilizers is often the cause.

Fig. 46. Tipping the pot this way decreases the force of the water flow from the drainage holes.

Illness must be judged on the basis of the plant's conditions, and suitable measures must be taken. For conditions involving the roots, repotting and elimination of the cause of trouble by means of application of chemicals are necessary. Chemical treatment of visible sickness on branches and trunks will solve the problem, but in all cases, use of only thoroughly disinfected—dried in the sunlight—soil is imperative.

9. IMPROPER CONTAINER

Pots with small surface area and great depth impair proper drainage, and very shallow pots, because of water tension, do not drain well. Glazing on porcelain obstructs ventilation. But with a certain ingenuity, even such containers can be used. For instance, tilting shallow containers (Fig. 46) reduces water tension and improves drainage. To increase ventilation in glazed porcelain pots, line them with sphagnum moss before planting; use coarse earth in deep, narrow containers. If the drainage hole in the bottom of the pot is too small, enlarge it.

10. DANGER OF METALS

Always avoid the use of steel or copper screens over the drainage hole in the container, and do not use bare copper wire to wrap trunks and branches or to secure plants in place. The oxidization of metals has surprisingly bad effects on plants.

11. SEVERELY WEAKENED PLANTS

Extreme cases of infirmity require thorough basic corrective steps and long periods of treatment. When this stage of advanced age and weakness has been reached, only the greatest attention to details will preserve a tree's life.

The first measures to take are the following. Using a water spray capable of generating considerable force, wash away all grime and soot from leaves, branches, and trunk. Next, if the soil in the container is unsuitable or exhausted, remove as much of it as possible, and replace it with clean soil.

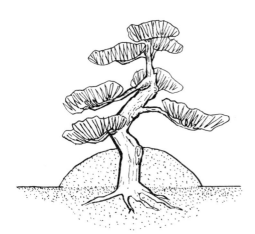

Fig. 47. Deep planting in the garden restores to vigor a tree in poor condition.

Fig. 48. Restoration treatment in a large pot or box. The bottom layer of soil is very coarse, the middle one of moderate coarseness. On top of this is spread sphagnum moss, and on top of that is sprinkled some fine soil.

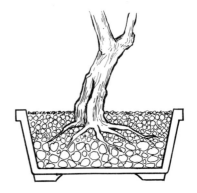

Remember, however, that pines and other evergreens will not tolerate total soil removal. Since a temperature of roughly eighteen degrees Centigrade (sixty-four degrees Fahrenheit) should be maintained, carry out these operations in early spring, or employ artificial means of establishing moderate warmth.

The plant may be kept in its original container if your garden has a shaded, well ventilated, dimly lighted corner for recuperation. If it lacks such a place, however, use a larger pot or box, for which you must make very careful drainage preparations. Although the portability of these containers permits transferring the plant to an environment similar to its natural one, they usually do not drain well. To remedy the situation use a large percentage of sand and a coarse earth in the soil mixture.

Weakened plants fall victim to many types of harm and illness, and their conditions are further aggravated if dry winds promote excess evaporation from leaves and resulting withering. To prevent this, water the leaves well to maintain a high humidity level, but take care that only moderate amounts of water reach the roots. Bear in mind the fact that in weakened conditions, plant roots become nearly inactive; consequently, care similar to that used for grafts cuttings—slightly dry roots, heavy leaf watering—contributes greatly to rapid recovery.

Premature fertilizing is dangerous to damaged plants, but a weak fertilizer solution poured over the leaves is effective.

Finally, all of these recuperative measures should be taken in spring or early summer, when the plant is most active: but they may be carried out at other seasons if the plant's condition warrants. Of course, badly afflicted plants require maximum protection.

126 CARE

5 Cultivation Guide

1. Five-needle Pine

Of the three kinds of five-needle pine—*Hime-komatsu*, from the high mountains of southern Japan; *Kita-goyomatsu*, from the high mountains of central Japan; and the *Hai-matsu*—the first is the most often used in bonsai, the second frequently treated as moderate-size bonsai, and the last never used at all. Trees with short, straight, well lined needles are most highly prized.

Although in the ancient past, cultivators took most of their five-needle pines from the mountains, today the scarcity of suitable small plants makes it necessary to use seedlings or grafts from large trees, plant them in open fields until they begin to grow well, and then pot them as bonsai.

The five-needle pine is easy to care for and requires repotting only once every four or five years, either at the vernal or autumnal equinox. Young plants bud so freely that it is sometimes necessary to trim the plants leaving only five or six base needles on each branch. Wiring should take place from December to February, and the trees should be moderately watered and kept in a sunny place. If a larger percentage of sand is used and if the soil is packed fairly firmly, the trees will bud less vigorously. Five-needle pines like good ventilation and strong sunlight.

2. Black and Red Pines

Masculine, powerful black and *nishiki* pines (*Pinus corticosa* Makino, a variety of black pine), largely from the seaside are balanced by the more feminine red pines of the northern mountains. The so-called *aiguro*, from the regions between the sea and the north, is neuter in feeling. Rough, ringed trunk bark is the characteristic of the best black pines from southern Japan (Kyushu and Shikoku). Young and vigorous trees bud well; therefore, in May or April, cut away all new buds—strong and weak alike—to promote a second crop of buds with shorter needles the same year. It is also possible to carefully fertilize plants with weak buds, cut the buds (nip red pines in August and black pines in September), and then wait till the following year for the second crop of shorter needles.

Because these pines have good root spreads, repotting, in late March, once every three or four years is sufficient. The soil should be sandy. Fertilize well, and water somewhat more heavily than in the case of five-needle

Fig. 49. Black pine.

pines. Although the black and *nishiki* pines prefer strong sunlight, the red pine will thrive in slightly more shady surroundings. Corrective wiring should be done from December to February, and although trimming excess foliage is often necessary, branches and needles must never be cut in cold weather.

3.   Silver Spruce and Sakhalin Spruce

Relying now almost totally on grafts and layering cultivators practically never use specimens of these trees taken from nature. Most of the spruces are highly sensitive to soot and dirt, but the bushy dense Sakhalin spruce (*Picea Glehni* Mast.) is popular bonsai material.

Repotting is necessary only about once in five or six years, and soil should be less sandy and lighter than that used for pines. Standard watering with plenty of sprinkling on the leaves is important. Fertilize well, and watch carefully for plant lice. Repotting should take place at either the vernal or the autumnal equinox and wiring from December to February. Although cuttings may be made either in late February or in July, after the new leaves are fully developed, their root generation is generally very poor. On the other hand, layering, though time consuming, produces vigorous trees with good shapes and fine root spreads.

4.   Japanese Cypress, Cryptomeria Cedar, Juniper, Sawara False Cypress (*Chamaecyparis pisifera*), and Chinese Juniper

Though the only one native to rocky mountainous terrain, the Chinese juniper resembles all the others in the group in most respects. Since in nature these trees tend to develop vast, straight trunks, they are most frequently found in single or double, straight-trunk-style bonsai. Furthermore, their rapid rate of growth makes possible extensive cultivation from cuttings.

They are fond of water and, if in good condition, require repotting only once in three or four years. Repot in either mid-April or at approximately the time of the autumnal equinox, but never during cold weather. The same is true of wiring and the other bonsai training operations. Protective shelter is required in cold climates, and all shaping and repotting must wait until the winter leaves have turned to spring leaves: that is, until the weather is warm.

Plenty of water, especially on the leaves, and good fertilization are important. Vigorous budding makes bud trimming essential, but since the leaves and needles are arranged on top of each other, scissors or even fingernails will damage the remaining foliage. Consequently, use only the fleshy part of the fingers in nipping buds. Pruning should be restricted to one-third the total foliage, and both pruning and bud nipping should be performed twice between the vernal and autumnal equinoxes. Soil should be either half sand and half earth or slightly more soil than sand. The Chinese junipers and other junipers, however, native to sandy soil, prefer extra lime. Thorough and repeated use of insecticides and plant disinfectants is essential to protect the plants from the leaf miner and the red withering disease, to which they are highly susceptible.

5. Maples

Especially beautiful in autumn and spring, the maples are strong and easy to care for. They require repotting with a larger percentage of soil than sand, only once every two or three years, at approximately the vernal equinox. Abundant budding makes nipping (at the vernal equinox) necessary; wiring and trimming should be performed during the early summer—the Japanese rainy season. It is possible to repot after pruning, but careful fertilizing must precede this operation. Though they require more time, the best maple bonsai are made from layered natural trees. Maples are hardy and do not suffer from the cold, but it is nonetheless wise to keep them in a protective shelter in the winter. Avoid spring pruning because by then the sap has risen and will flow out of the wounds and cause a serious loss of tree strength. In addition, never repot once the new leaves are out and fully opened.

Carefully trim all vigorous buds and those growing from the sides of branches to insure the delicate, soft quality in the branch ends prized in these plants. Water and fertilize them well, and restrict the amount of direct sunlight to which they are subjected by storing them in half-shade.

6. Zelkova, Chinese Nettle, Beech, Elm, Carpinus, and Birch

Another group of the most representative deciduous trees taken from, or near, the high mountains, these please the eye especially because of their

Fig. 50. Birch.

beautiful autumn colors and the delicate grace of their branches. The most hardy, the zelkova, requires ample fertilizer and thorough bud trimming. (The beech, however, must never be pruned.)

Although the period may be as long as two or three years, the zelkova may also be repotted every year, at the vernal or autumnal equinoxes. Furthermore, if they are pruned during the early summer rainy weather, they may be repotted at the same time, just as is the case with the maples. The fast growing zelkova demand repeated trimmings, clipping, and pruning, and frequent fertilizing to prevent long branches from developing and spoiling the shape. Their soil should be more earth than sand and should contain compost and a soil with high-moisture retention. Though they are hardy in cold weather, bonsai zelkova should be stored in protective shelters to prevent direct contact with frost and consequent root freezing. Similarly, these trees can tolerate plenty of sunlight, but over-exposure can scorch the leaves. They must be protected from the hot afternoon western sun.

What has been said of the zelkova holds true for all the other trees in this group.

7. The Waxtree Group

These trees are most prized for their autumn foliage, but in the spring when their new buds develop, they can be injurious to people who are alergic to lacquer.

They will not tolerate dryness in winter, and they should be repotted after the vernal equinox, when the new buds have already developed. Store them in sunny places. Most training and corrective work must be done in spring or summer, but since even old branches produce abundant buds, pruning and shaping is virtually unrestricted. Even branches as old as two or three years may be cut with impunity. Well fertilized trees need transplanting only once in two or three years; soil should be largely earthy. Watering follows standard bonsai procedures except for two points. The trees must never dry out during the winter, and the cultivator must be careful not to touch the plant because the leaves contain a rash-producing poison.

8. Wintercreeper (*Euonymus fortunei*)

The polished luster of their leaves and the brocade-like beauty of their autumn foliage make these plants great bonsai favorites. Since they are southern in origin, they require shelter and protection in winter. Using largely earthy soils, repot them after the vernal equinox. Carefully trim their buds, and prune and wire them during the rainy weather of early summer. Severe pruning is possible at that time is one-third of the foliage is left for the sake of water intake. Both their fragrant blossoms and their berries harmonize with the feeling of summer. Though they are easily grown from cuttings, the process requires as much as six or seven years. Water and fertilize them well, store them in moderately shady places out of the western sun, and put them in protective winter shelter earlier than most other bonsai.

9. Evergreen Oak and Konara Oak (*Quercus serrata*)

These plants are most enjoyed for their large, pale green, soft, early spring leaves and for the charm of their foliage tossed in summer breezes. In addition, however, the few leaves persistently clinging to the branches in winter picturesquely highlight the changing of the seasons. Both easy to raise and hardy, they should be repotted after the vernal equinox, and their soil should contain a little more sand than is usual for deciduous trees. If well fertilized, they need be repotted only once in two or three years. Water them well, and store them out of the western sun in shady places to prevent leaf scorching. They require good ventilation. Wire them in the early summer rainy weather, and after fertilizing, prune them. The amount of foliage cut away must not exceed one-third of the total.

10. Ginkgo

This unusual tree, which reaches vast sizes in nature, is prized for its formal beauty, its fresh green spring and dazzling gold autumnal foliage, and especially for its nuts and its habit of producing aerial roots. Though hardy, since the ginkgo will not tolerate freezing, it must be stored in a shelter in winter. Repotting, using more earthy soil and less sand, should be done once in two or three years, after the vernal equinox, when the buds have opened. Watering procedures are standard. The straight trunk and branches need little wiring, but pruning and bud trimming should be done in the early summer rainy weather. Ginkgo may be grown from seeds, cuttings, or layers of mature trees. For best results cuttings should be taken before the new buds open and should be dried in the sun one or two days before planting. Fertilize the ginkgo well, and take extra precautions to protect its delicate bark from damage.

11. Japanese Torreya (*Torreya nucifera*) and Hemlock Spruce

Bonsai versions of these plants must reveal the same straight, tall forms that occur in nature. Repot once every three or four years with half earthy soil and half sand; the best season is from the vernal equinox till the rainy early part of the summer, but the plants must not be repotted until the buds are open and the new leaves firmly established (until after May). Water well, especially the surfaces of the leaves, and fertilize amply. Lack of fertilizing results in a poor second crop of buds after the first have been trimmed. Extremely hardy, these plants survive cold as long as they are not exposed to frost. Weak plants, however, naturally require protection. Cuttings are surprisingly easy to take, and layering produces excellent bonsai.

12. Winged Spindle Tree (*Euonymus alatus*) and Spindle Tree

These trees both vie with the maples for autumnal-foliage honors and develop interesting clusters of berries. Soil for repotting—once every two or three years, after the vernal equinox—should be largely earthy and should contain about ten per cent compost. Fertilize well, water often, especially the foliage, and in summer store in the shade. Since these are fruit-bearing plants, only a few of the early buds can be trimmed. Pruning must be done before the spring buds appear, and wiring and other corrective steps must be taken in the early summer rainy weather. Because they grow vigorously and spread roots fast and well, they must never be allowed to dry out during the growing season. Furthermore, ample fertilizing is essential in the summer to prevent desiccation of branches in the winter. Extremely sensitive to cold, these trees must be protected in freezing weather. If leaves become very dirty in the summer, it is possible to prune them. Do not trim buds too heavily as this destroys the tree's ability to bloom and produce fruit. (Bittersweet is cared for in the same manner.)

13. Plums

Harbinger of spring, blooming when there are no other flowers, the plum is so popular a garden plant that it has been the subject of countless variations and developments. Repotting, necessary once every two or three years, must not be done at the spring equinox, when the trees blossom, but must wait until after the flowers have fallen. The soil should be mostly earthy and should contain about twenty per cent compost. Plums like sunlight and dryness, but they nevertheless require ample watering. An atomizer spray of water on the branches especially when the plant is in bud, promotes good flowering. Fertilize well with a preponderance of animal matter such as fish meal. Prune after the flowers have dropped, but since there is a bud at the leaf base of every new branch, do not cut severely once the buds have grown large. Of course, you must shape the plant on the basis of the positions of the new branches, but trim their ends lightly. Badly misshapen branches can be wired into position during the wet season of early summer.

During hot, humid weather use disinfectants and insecticides to rid the plants of cockroaches, mildew, and downy mildew.

14. Japanese Quince and Chinese Quince

Japanese quince, popular for its flowers, and Chinese quince, most admired for its fruit, are both very popular bonsai materials. The Japanese plant comes in many varieties and colors—red, white, orange-red, pink—and blooms well with long-lasting flowers. One variety blooms once in each season of the year. Spring repotting, though it will not bring about a sudden failure in the plant's condition, does lower its resistance to disease. Consequently, repot at about the autumnal equinox. These strong plants, if well fertilized, need repotting no more than once every four or five years. Because the flowering season is long, at about the vernal equinox, pluck the

Fig. 51. Japanese quince.

flowers, and prune thoroughly, bearing in mind the necessity of sparing the reserve buds, just as is the case with plums.

Although young or vigorous trees may be pruned and wired during the early summer rainy weather, ample fertilizing is essential to keep them in good condition. During the period of active growth, buds grow fast, but severe pruning will force the plant to put out another crop of buds and thus to sacrifice good blossoms. To avoid this, leave intact many of the branches that grow in the summer. Animal fertilizer is best.

In general, the Chinese quince is treated as the other deciduous trees, but since both it and the Japanese quince bud early, the tendency is to repot them earlier. This must not be done, however, before the vernal equinox.

Store these plants in sunny places, and water and fertilize well. They should be planted in largely earthy soil, but be careful to guard against the crown gall, to which the roots of these plants are susceptible. Because they bloom while the weather is still cold, it is best to enjoy them indoors.

15. Cherry, Peach, and Aronia

Bonsai versions of the cherry, the most beloved of Japanese springtime flowers, are rare because, though the tree is hardy, it does not live long. Cherries from southern regions are the most popular for bonsai purposes because they bloom earlier. Repotting, required after the vernal equinox, once every two or three years, involves removal of all the old soil and replacing it with new. The work may also be done after the autumnal equinox and before the leaves fall. Wiring is best done in the early summer rainy weather after the new branches are well established, but trimming must be light. In summer, protect the trees from scorching by keeping them in a well ventilated, shady place, and in winter, put them in protective shelters. Since they fall victim fast to many diseases, frequent and careful disinfection is a vital point.

Use earthy soil that drains well. Since the bark is delicate, take special care to disinfect all scratches or wounds.

Although the aronia, bonsai of which are more numerous, is hardier than the cherry, the two share one important point in common. Unless both are repotted earlier in the spring, the chances of loosing the plant are great. No matter how well rooted a plant seems, when repotting is needed, do not hesitate.

16. Winter-flowering Yellow Jasmine and Forsythia

The most important of the none-too-numerous bonsai plants with yellow flowers is the winter-flowering yellow jasmine. Blooming early in the spring while still in the protective shelter, the jasmine is a source of joy to the cultivator. The forsythia has tender young leaves that make its yellow flowers even more charming.

Native to warm climates, these plants require winter protection. Repotting, required only once every two or three years, should be done after

Fig. 52. Winter-flowering yellow jasmine.

either the vernal or the autumnal equinox. Potting soil should be largely earthy. Fertilize well. As is true of most flowering plants, they should be lightly trimmed when in bud and thoroughly pruned after the flowers have dropped. Water well, and in summer keep them in a place that becomes shady early in the afternoon. Propagation is easy, since both trees make good cuttings and layers.

17. Gardenia

The chief charms of the plant are its fragrant white flowers, its evergreen leaves, and red autumn berries. Of the many regional variations in leaf and berry shape, the roundest forms of both are most hightly prized. Gardenias make good cuttings. Blooming in the early summer rainy season, the ordinary repotting time, gardenias should be repotted at about the autumnal equinox, once every three or four years. Unless a greenhouse is available, spring repotting is dangerous since the tree is susceptible to cold.

Use earthy soil, and water often. Fertilize well, and keep in a sunny area that becomes shady early in the afternoon. No matter how well rooted, all gardenia bonsai should be given protective shelter in winter. Use some of the good modern agricultural chemicals to rid these plants of the scale insects that plague them.

18. Azaleas (*Rhododendron indicum* and *Rhododendron lateritium*)

One of the oldest and most widely admired of all flowering bonsai azaleas are available in colors ranging from white through red to mauve, and sometimes skillful cultivators contrive to force all these colors to bloom on one plant. Naturally, since it has many hundreds of years of tradition and occurs in numerous varieties, the azalea bonsai is also the subject of a great deal of convention, but I prefer to treat it in a modern way.

A coarse pumice soil is considered best for these plants. For old trees or those recently brought in from the mountains and lacking sufficient roots, mix sphagnum moss with pumice soil to about twenty or thirty per cent. Pruning should take place no later than about July 15, or buds for the following year's flowers will not form. When repotting, once every three or four years, remove no more than about two-thirds of the root mass. Fertilize well, except when the plant is in flower. Azaleas are victim to many insects, particularly to the red louse, from the damage of which they often wither and die. Afflicted plants must be sprayed with insecticide three or four times at intervals of three or four days. Other insects which eat and destroy the buds also afflict azaleas and must be destroyed on sight.

These plants like both sunlight and plenty of water, especially on their leaves. Since their rootlets approach the surface of the soil, it is a good idea to spread a carpet of moss for protection. Corrective wiring should be done during the rainy part of the summer, but since the trunks of the plants are sensitive, wrap the wire in paper before applying it. Azaleas require only moderate winter protection.

19. Pomegranates and Crepe Myrtle

The many pomegranate varieties are popular because they are lovely without their leaves, with them, and especially when they bloom white, red, yellow, pink, crimson, or variegated flowers.

Repotting, once every three or four years, requires earthy soil with a mixture of twenty or thirty per cent pumice soil, and ten per cent compost. It should take place either after the vernal equinox when the buds have appeared or after pruning in the early-summer rainy weather. In summer, prevent leaf scorching by keeping the plants in the shade. Fertilize and water well, especially the surfaces of the leaves; and prune in early spring before the buds appear. After they are out, no more work should be done until the flowers bloom. This happens in the rainy part of early summer or mid-summer, the time for wiring the plant, if needed. Remove these plants to protective shelter early because they are extremely sensitive to cold.

20. Wisteria

A tree with long trailing vine-like branches, the wisteria's unusual form and distinctive blossoms make handsome bonsai.

When repotting, once every two or three years, remove all of the pot soil, but take great care not to cut any of the large roots. Soil should be largely earthy with an admixture of compost or ten or twenty per cent of pumice soil. Because it grows fast, the wisteria needs both ample fertilizing and plenty of water, especially in the summer when the danger of drying increases. Flowers develop on the branches that do not trail far; consequent-

Fig. 53. Rose.

ly, prune only those that run to excess lengths. During the winter, protect the plant from both direct exposure to frost and from drying.

21. Roses

Bonsai fanciers generally prize old, wild roses, with interesting, thick trunks, glossy leaves, and small, inconspicuous flowers; but cultivated roses that produce a similar effect are suitable. Using a mixture of earthy soil and ten or twenty per cent compost, repot once every two or three years in the early spring. Keep them in well ventilated, sunny places, and water them in the standard fashion. Fertilize well, and trim off new branches and stalks early because their sudden growth causes older ones to wither. As is often the case with bonsai, guard roses from direct contact with the frost and from drying in the winter.

22. Magnolias, Thurber's Magnolia (*Magnolia Kobus*), and *Amelanchier asiatica*

Both the large-flowered white and magenta magnolias and the Thurber's magnolia, bursting into bloom without warning, are popular forerunners of springtime.

Immediately after the flowers have fallen, once every two or three years, repot using mostly earthy soil. Fertilize well, and protect the plants from the hot, western summer sun because their leaves scorch easily. Limited in the number of branches they produce, these plants should be pruned only after the flowers have dropped and buds should be nipped moderately to stimulate the growth of as many branches as possible. Using paper-wrapped wire to protect the delicate bark, wire the plants during the early-summer rainy weather. In winter, store in a protective shelter, and guard against drying.

The more hardy *Amelanchier asiatica* may be thoroughly wired during the summer rainy weather and its branches lightly trimmed if fertilizer is applied in ample quantity.

23. Camellias, Sasanqua, and Fragrant Olive

Unfortunately because of their often unattractive tree shapes, these plants, of which there are many old and handsome blooming varieties, find scant application in bonsai. Nonetheless, the elegant single-flowering varieties add a splash of bright color to a bonsai collection.

Using earthy soil, repot annually in April or May immediately after the flowers have dropped, and be careful not to cut the large roots. In summer, keep in a well ventilated place out of the hot western sun. Do not trim buds; instead, correct shapes by pruning. Paper-wrapped wire may be applied in May or June, but it should be removed as quickly as possible. These trees will survive the winter easily if they are protected from direct exposure to frost and are suitably watered. Although they like fertilizing, never apply large doses at one time. Be especially cautious of insects, to which these trees are very susceptible.

The autumn-flowering fragrant olive is attractive, but since it fares poorly in urban conditions it is little used for bonsai. Its care, however, is identical with that of the camellias.

Fig. 54. Sasanqua.

24. Silk Tree, Japanese Wisteria, and *Milletia japonica*

Some people are fond of these trees because their flowers seem to invite summer breezes. The blossoms of the silk tree are red; those of the *Milletia japonica* are white. All are hardy and take root fast.

Using earthy soil, repot once every two or three years at about the vernal equinox. Remove all the old soil, but do not cut the large roots. Fertilize and water the silk tree well, protect it from the hot summer sun, and watch carefully for insects and diseases, to which these trees are often victims. Pruning must be held to a minimum, but paper-wrapped wire may be used to correct shapes of soft new branches. Especially sensitive to cold, these plants require careful winter protection.

The *Milletia japonica* should be kept in sunny, well ventilated places, and pruned once before the buds appear and once again after the flowers have fallen. Fertilize well, and guard against cold and drying in winter.

25. Willows and Tamarisk

The most popular of all summer bonsai, the weeping willow and the tamarisk, with their gracefully hanging branches, suggest the coolness of a waterside bank, even on hot, humid days. Because they are strong and grow fast, they must be repotted once every year or two, at about the time of the vernal equinox. Use earthy soil. Pruning before the new buds appear promotes the development of stronger branches; therefore, it should be thorough and even a little severe. Remove all unnecessary branches, and bend the others into the desired positions with your fingertips. New tamarisk branches, which tend to grow upward, should be wired into hanging positions in the rainy part of the early summer, but because they assume position quickly, the wiring may be loose and must be removed quickly. Fertilize and water abundantly, and store in sunny, well ventilated places in summer. Thinned chemical insecticides will often rid these plants of the cockroaches that pester them. Since they suffer severely from the cold, they must be given thorough winter protection, and pruning must under no circumstances be attempted before early spring.

26. Dwarfed Kumquat, Horned Orange, and Shaddock

Despite extreme difficulties in producing good shapes with these fruit-bearing plants, the dwarfed kumquat, because of its dense branches, occurs frequently in bonsai. The horned orange too is popular because of the unusual shape of its fruit. Since they grow fast, are hardy, and take root well, they require repotting once every two years with earthy soil. Fertilize them well, and keep them in sunny, well ventilated places. Until the fruit develops, bud trimming must be light. After the fruit has fallen, however, prune thoroughly. Using paper-wrapped material, wire in the rainy part of early summer, but remove the wire as soon as possible since the barks of these plants are fragile. Complete protection and suitable watering are essential to assist these plants in surviving the winter.

27. Aronia, Apple, and Pear

The aronia, which comes in four or five flowering and fruit-bearing varieties, is naturally a bonsai favorite. The apple and the pear, of course, bloom handsomely, but their fruit is their major source of interest.

Hardy and easy to care for, these trees require repotting once every two or three years, at the vernal equinox. Use earthy soil with an admixture of ten or twenty per cent compost. Spring repotting produces a bad crop of fruit that year; consequently, to avoid this it is possible to repot the plants at the autumnal equinox if they are then well fertilized. Keep them in well ventilated sunny places, fertilize amply, and in the rainy season spray frequently with insecticides and disinfectants to guard against pests and diseases, to which these trees are special victims. Avoid severe pruning because both flowers and fruit develop from the buds of old branches. Wire with paper-covered wire in the rainy part of the early summer, but take precautions not to damage the bark because wounds lead immediately to disease. For winter protection, guard against direct frost exposure, and during repotting, never cut the large roots.

28. Ilex

Beloved for its bright red berries, ilex is one of the best of all autumnal bonsai. Since it roots quickly, repot with earthy soil once every year or two at about the vernal equinox. Do not damage the main roots. Keep in a well ventilated, sunny place, and fertilize well until the tree blooms. At this point stop fertilizing until the berries have formed. Water well to avoid sudden loss of leaf color and cessation of growth. Trim off unwanted buds early, and take special care to give full protection from cold and drying in the winter.

29. Persimmon

The glowing golden orbs and black branches of this tree are one of the loveliest autumn sights Japan has to offer. Although it hates having its large roots cut and being transplanted, the persimmon must be repotted once every three or four years. Using earthy soil, carry out the operation in early spring, taking extra care not to damage the roots. Water well. Fertilize abundantly until the plant blooms; then moderate the amounts applied until after the fruit has formed. It is difficult to stimulate a crop of fruit in the year in which the plant has been repotted.

Prune in early spring before the buds appear, and wire carefully with paper-covered materials during the rainy part of early summer. Water well, keep in sunny, well ventilated places, and guard against exposure to frost in winter.

Index